THE
USA

THE USA

IVAN T. SANDERSON
and the Editors of Country Beautiful

Published by
COUNTRY BEAUTIFUL
CORPORATION
Waukesha, Wisconsin

Distributed by
RAND MC NALLY
& COMPANY

Dawn over the fog-shrouded Colorado foothills.

COUNTRY BEAUTIFUL: *Publisher and Editorial Director:* Michael P. Dineen; *Executive Editor:* Robert L. Polley: *Managing Editor:* Charles R. Fowler; *Contributing Editors:* Joseph Dever, William Bibber, Peter Barnicle, James Droney; *Senior Editors:* Kenneth L. Schmitz, James H. Robb; *Assistant Art Director:* Robert Fehring; *Editorial Assistant:* Joseph M. Treen; *Distribution:* Bernard J. Connell, Mel Rozier, John Dineen; *Administration:* B. Robert Peck, Sharon G. Armao; *Assistants:* Trudy Schnittka, Kathleen Kons.

The Editors are grateful to the following publishers for permission to include the following copyright material in this volume: Holt, Rinehart and Winston, Inc., for excerpt from "The Gift Outright" from COMPLETE POEMS OF ROBERT FROST. Copyright 1942 by Robert Frost. Reprinted by permission of Holt, Rinehart and Winston, Inc. Holt, Rinehart and Winston, Inc., for excerpt from "Stopping by Woods on a Snowy Evening" from COMPLETE POEMS OF ROBERT FROST. Copyright 1923 by Holt, Rinehart and Winston, Inc. Copyright 1951 by Robert Frost. Reprinted by permission of Holt, Rinehart and Winston, Inc. Alfred A. Knopf, Inc., for excerpts from DEMOCRACY IN AMERICA. Copyright 1945 by Alfred A. Knopf, Inc. Reprinted by permission of the publisher of DEMOCRACY IN AMERICA, by Alexis de Tocqueville, translated by Phillips Bradley.

Country Beautiful Corporation is a wholly owned subsidiary of Flick-Reedy Corporation: President: Frank Flick; Vice President and General Manager: Michael P. Dineen; Treasurer and Secretary: August Caamano.

CONTENTS

Family group at Lake Michigan shoreline.

INTRODUCTION

A Land of Wonders

The United States themselves are essentially the greatest
poem. Here at last is something in the doings of man that cor-
responds with the broadcast doings of the day and night . . . .
—— Walt Whitman, Preface to *Leaves of Grass*

This is a book about America. It is about her land, her history, her
achievements, her people and her future. It is about the oldest republic in the world which is also one of the younger nations. It is an attempt
to capture the spirit and the accomplishments of a people that in less than
200 years has come from an uncertain experiment to be a model for, and
leader of, much of the world — despite, but also because of its diversity,
and, we might add, because of its stubbornness and its optimism.

It is, appropriately enough, in the spirit of this last quality — optimism — that this volume has been written. For, on the whole, America
has not substantially changed since 1835, when the Frenchman, Alexis de
Tocqueville, wrote in his book, *Democracy in America:*

"They [the Americans] have all a lively faith in the perfectability of
man, they judge that the diffusion of knowledge must necessarily be ad-
vantageous, and the consequences of ignorance fatal; they all consider society as a body in a state of improvement, humanity as a changing scene in
which nothing is, or ought to be, permanent; and they admit that what
appears to them today to be good, may be superseded by something
better tomorrow."

Optimism is not usually a noticeable characteristic of books today;
and the problems of America — surviving racial injustice, pockets of poverty, the strain of violence in the popular culture — cannot be ignored.
But our emphasis will be the "poem," as Walt Whitman wrote, that *is*
America; the country that de Tocqueville spoke of when he wrote:

"America is a land of wonders, in which everything is in constant motion and every change seems an improvement. The idea of novelty is there indissolubly connected with the idea of amelioration. No natural boundary seems to be set to the efforts of man; and in his eyes what is not yet done is only what he has not yet attempted to do."

"Every man," Thomas Jefferson wrote, "has two countries — his own and France." A young African author recently changed this to read "his own and America," for the United States has come to be just what her Founding Fathers had hoped she would become — an example to all other peoples of just what *can* be done. The ability to gather such momentum in so many areas of endeavor, while at the same time contending with so many contradictions and problems, and so many streams of activity going in so many different directions — has much to do with America's attraction for others and is what prompts them to examine, analyze and learn from the American experience.

It is characteristic of nations which are directed by dictators or ideologies to drive ahead in one or two areas with single-minded purpose, to make swift gains and occasionally to produce spectacular, but isolated triumphs. However, and especially in recent centuries, such inflexible, narrowly directed nations do not long retain their impetus and do not often live up to their early promise.

The only alternative foundation upon which a nation can be built is that of an "open" democratic society. In the short view, such a society — it is too complex to call a "system" — is often regarded as too haphazard, considerably inefficient and far too slow in action. In America, however, the nurturing of individual freedom and equal opportunity has produced a continuous and progressive social and economic "flowering" which has eliminated the need for violent change and given us the abundant life envisaged by the signers of the Declaration of Independence, and forever sought by all mankind. Although all manner of new problems and tests must inevitably lie ahead, as long as we preserve individual freedom and continue to widen opportunity for all, there is no reason to be pessimistic. Our current problems would be terrifying and perhaps overwhelming to others, but America is tackling them frontally in the sincere belief that our "system" is the best yet devised.

Certainly those who read of the wonders of America can have little doubt that her faith in "progress" has been justified; while Americans, although they don't like to admit the fact, still retain the old feeling that the mountains which stand so beautifully in the distance, touched here by

(Continued on page 15)

Humboldt Peak, Colorado Rockies.

Dancer's silhouette.

Miami skyline at twilight.

Poppy fields, southern California.

Church, New Hampshire.

Air Force Academy Chapel, Colorado.

Lincoln Memorial, Washington, D. C.

Suburban homes, Sun City, Arizona.

Absaroka Range, Wyoming.

glints of sunlight and there by shadows of clouds, are indeed the "Delectable Mountains" of John Bunyan's *Pilgrim's Progress,* the immortal book many early settlers carried with them to these shores.

True freedom and prosperity have flowered on a continent that is, for the most part, alternately fertile and sterile in a rigid round of the seasons and where, from the beginning, scarcity was usually balanced with plenty. If the turkeys were few, the fish were many; and, when the corn lay withered, plump deer scurried through the forest or herds of buffalo thundered across the plains. When the Eastern farmlands were all under cultivation, ships and railroads opened up vast new areas; and when the industrial revolution took hold, our people, with unsurpassed energy and ingenuity, further multiplied the nation's bounty. Finally, when world leadership was going a-begging, America rose to the challenge.

It needs to be remembered that natural abundance — and thus plenitude of goods and power — are basically Nature's gifts to many nations. Many nations, however, have made little or no use of these. America, on the other hand, seems from the beginning to have had a vision of itself as an "unfinished" land and one which will always remain, at least partially, an undiscovered land.

Many diverse factors have contributed to the present greatness of this country. The land itself, still virtually a virgin colossus when the first European colonists arrived, was pregnant with riches. Yet, it was the spirit and the energy, the initiative and the enterprise, and the very souls within those who came here that brought this slumbering giant to life. Not only poets and writers, but artists in every other field conceived by man, have flowered here as never before in history. This is a God-fearing nation and devout, whatever be the individual's Faith, and this has given it strength. But perhaps, above all, it is its entirely unique and homegrown form of government that has brought this miracle into being. Freedom is its keynote and its keystone but, while it is called a democracy, it has neither roots in, nor any resemblance to, the slave-based states of ancient Greece that were so named. The best way to explain just what our system is, is to say that "Americans govern themselves." This concept was the genius of those who wrote our Constitution, and for it we should be everlastingly grateful.

It is in gratitude that this book endeavors to pay tribute to this treasured land.

Interlaced branches form a pattern of trees.

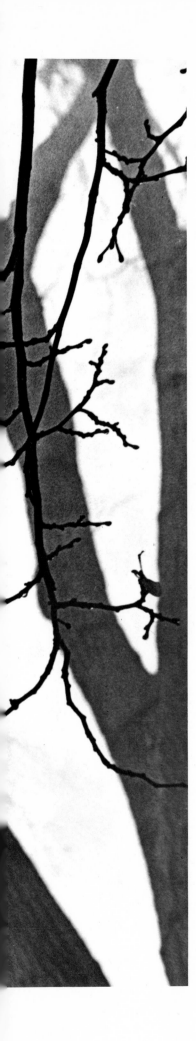

The Gifts of the Land

I

The American Forests: Of Time and Trees

The east and west borders of the American continent are brushed by tireless oceans, the land between a vast panorama of cities and urban sprawls, farms centered in the checkerboard of pastures and fenced fields of grain, uninhabited deserts and deep canyons laced with rushing, white rivers and forests as far as the eye can see.

That is America today. But to understand anything of her past we must first dwell on the forest. The forest was the most pervasive physical fact that confronted the first European settlers of the East Coast. It helped to shape their lives as it had permeated the culture of many Indian tribes who had possessed the continent for centuries before. Time and progress have changed that fact, but the forest remains, perhaps in a secondary role, yet an essential and living link with our past and a vital and enduring sustenance for our people today.

Forests that once totaled well over a billion acres now add up to about 700 million acres of trees — some standing in natural perpetuity in areas such as northern Maine and others being carefully nurtured toward maturity in places where man once abused the land beyond its tolerance. There are mist-mantled conifers holding firm in the Blue Ridge Mountains; the surrealistic evergreens of Pacific California struggling against the sea and wind; and lush vegetation springing from dark and placid swamps in Florida and Louisiana. Collectively, each scene is a bit of America's heritage and her wealth — still one of the nation's greatest natural resources.

And time and progress continue to work their patterns, changing the face of the land. The peaceful New England farm of the 1930's, a scant 35 miles from Boston, has been obliterated, the owner's woodlot and fields and pastures scraped away to make room for the ceaseless real estate developments and the urge of Americans to escape to be nearer the trees they are destroying.

On Manhattan Island there is not a single tree alive of the forests which greeted the Dutch settlers. It's doubtful that today's Manhattan greenery,

Barren grounds caribou, Alaska.

*Migration of snow geese,
North Carolina.*

often tastefully scattered, was spawned from seeds wind-sown by ocean breezes brushing against the waving deciduous and conifer stands.

Concerned Americans have formed conservation commissions and taken other steps to preserve the heritage of the forest and its environs: In 1831 the Federal Government first forbid the cutting of trees on Federal lands; the American Tree Farm system was formed in 1941 to continue both the aesthetic and economical aspects of living lumber, a crop to be harvested wisely, but sown again so that tomorrow's generations might not be deprived of what has been taken away.

That to which we are giving a second birth was an awesome spectacle to those first visitors from Europe. Doubtless the Pilgrims stood in wonder as they looked upon the tall pines on the shores of Plymouth. The Jamestown Colony's historians wrote of the great forests which enveloped their first perilous years here.

The iron axe swung by a settler felled trees, then cut them into long logs. Notches were cut in opposite sides of each end and they were placed one atop the other until four walls filled a clearing in the forest. A neighbor, if there was one, would help lay up and peg the rafters in place, then short chunks of cedar were split with the same axe and the shingles placed upon the roof. Times were not easy, but Americans made the most of it, reaping the unhewn raw materials placed at their doorsteps by the forests.

The forest gave much—raw materials for homes, tools, flowers to grace rough, split-log tables—and harbored a wealth of food. There was no fear of it. In shaded glens knifed by rushing brooks, the settlers felled huge trees to dam the waters. More trees were cut and laboriously sliced into rough planks with unwieldy saws over a long trench called a sawyer's pit. The hardwood was fashioned into waterwheels with pegs and hand-cut nails so that grain could be ground into flour.

In a number of abandoned cellar holes scattered across New England can be found the remnants of utilitarian, primitive workmanship at its best. There are huge screws, a foot or more in diameter with deep threads hand-cut into the hard oak. The threaded portion is fitted into a heavy slab of wood, and at its bottom is a square panel forming the movable top of a massive handmade box. The settlers would gather apples and grind them in another all-wood machine. The dripping pulp was poured into the box and the screw turned down with a long lever. The juice was used for cider and preserves, the gifts of the rugged land complementing each other.

Before the Revolutionary War, the tallest, straightest trees which once filled the primeval forests were marked for the King of England with an axe. These were earmarked for shipmasts for the Royal Navy, and woe to the pioneer who cut one. Any fir or pine more than two feet in diameter was thus marked, and legend has it this is why the widest floorboards found in pre-Revolutionary New England homes never measure wider than 23 inches — a scant inch short of severe punishment for felling the King's property.

The giant trees are gone now, eradicated by unwitting woodsmen. Three thousand miles to the west are Pacific parallels to the former giants of the Northeast, the magnificent stands of trees, known as sequoias, whose trunks may measure 35 feet in diameter and have enough wood in a single tree to build 40 five-room homes. The trees grow up and up, their tips searching for sunlight above the shade cast by their fellows until they reach well over 200 feet. The largest and one of the oldest living things known to man is the General Sherman sequoia, containing 50,010 cubic feet and being 3,500 years old. The world's tallest trees are the famous Pacific Coast redwoods, another kind of sequoia, which sometimes exceed 350 feet.

The wonders of the forest have been many, and without them the first adventurers would certainly have turned their back on the New World. Without them, America would be less wealthy — in mind and spirit, as well as in material goods. For the wilderness is dear to every man and there is no wilderness to rival a wild forest.

Winter woods, northern Wisconsin.

Cracked soil.

Collecting maple syrup, Vermont.

Lighthouse, Maine.

Tens of thousands of gallons of maple syrup, that uniquely American product, are produced every year from the full-breasted trees covering the northeastern quarter of the country. The Indians made it by slashing the heavy-barked trees with an axe, collecting the sap in wooden troughs and boiling it in kettles made from the bark of the white, or canoe, birch. They learned they could reduce the water content of the sugar-rich sap by keeping the fire's temperature low, so low that the bark container would not burn. The settlers found the waxy fruit of the bayberry, and learned (again from the Indians) that when boiled in water, they could skim the surface and use the berry's protective coating for fragrant candles to light their log homes. The curious red and seemingly unpalatable cranberries sprang from sphagnum moss-filled swamps, creating an acid soil which made the tiny berries flourish. They made excellent preserves for the icy winters which stilled life for half a year at a time.

The gifts of the forest are extraordinary. Paper is made from pulp trees sawn in the 3,000-mile strip across the roof of America and in the Southeast; lumber builds the thousands of new homes erected each year; the chemical constituents of trees form useful products such as turpentine; boats to harvest the crops of the sea are built from it; and above all it is a vital link in the chain of life.

Today, as always, many Americans often feel in the forest an exhilaration, an expansion of their free spirit. Perhaps the forest has become a symbol of their frontier-conquering past. Or perhaps it simply is that the air is purer in forests because of the abundance of oxygen, that element which supports the lives of man and beast. Photosynthesis is necessarily a complex process, but suffice to say trees "inhale" carbon dioxide in the same manner mammals inhale oxygen. While man and animals gather oxygen in their lungs to support their lives and expel carbon dioxide, trees depend upon carbon dioxide and in turn "exhale" oxygen. Thus, the life of tree and man goes on. His life, as he knows it, would end the moment the last tree was felled.

Search any American city, and there are young trees growing; walk through the cruel-appearing devastation of a once-virgin forest cut for its timber, and there are seedlings sprouting. The bountiful redwoods of the West will be preserved, along with the primitive growths of the Southeast's swamps, the great deciduous varieties of the Great Smoky Mountains of North Carolina and Tennessee, the piny woods of the South, the noble coniferous growths of the northwoods and the Olympic rain forest of the Pacific Northwest.

To most Americans, the vast swamps appear to be a fearsome, prehistoric forest. Slash pines point to the sky, and mangroves and cypress thrus weird formations above the water. While the sequoia stands tall in mist-shaded mountains, the bald cypress is content to flourish in swampy land, virtually bottomless and seemingly an unfitting place for vegetation a hundred feet high.

The extraordinary appearance of the cypress is nature's engineering

Cypress swamp, Florida.

at its best, the compensation of creature for environment. The trunk's base spreads out at the water's surface, and there are strange "knees" thrust upwards in its perimeter, which appear as tiny stumps.

Even in these water-ridden forests the fury of nature extracts its price of life. For without man there would still be never-ending natural destruction. Fire can wreak more devastation on a forest in a day than man can in a year. It has happened for decades, centuries, eons — long before the match or cigarette was invented.

Some of the great forest fires of the American past are an indelible part of her history. The Peshtigo fire in Wisconsin and Michigan in 1871 burned 3,780,000 acres of timber and killed 1,638 people. The 1902 Yacolt fire of the Pacific Northwest destroyed 239,920 acres of forest, causing clouds of smoke so dense that people in the cities throughout the region had to keep lamps lit during the dark day.

It takes decades for the forest to replenish itself, but it will, with a forest of almost exactly the same kind. There are seeds of maples and oaks and ash and conifers buried beneath the rich carpet of humus, a natural layer of asbestos, if you will. Suddenly beneath the blackened spires of fire-raped oaks and maples and pines there is a stirring of life, a split in the soil appears and the green wisp of a seedling seeks the sun. There they will flourish, and shadow the dead ancestors until spring's waters and summer's heat rots their boles and they fall and decay to enrichen the black humus so that another generation of America's greatest heritage will live.

If there is an epilogue here, it is a testament of yesteryear. The most tiresome swaths of tract-homes in America are surrounded by green lawns, the rural farms circled with green. The new homeowner and the sun-scarred farmer alike struggle to make trees grow. It seems as if it were instinctive for Americans still to seek the forest.

Seashores, Lakes and Rivers: The Sweet Waters

Cape Cod, Cape Hatteras, Padre Island, Point Reyes — wherever the two great realms of land and water meet holds a peculiar fascination. No other landscape is as transitory in mood and exciting as the seacoast and no seashores as diverse as those of the American continent, and to the American it is a special place for it was his source. It was on the land that faces the sea that his forebears first touched this soil.

On the kelp-strewn beaches of the Bay of Fundy, off the northeast tip of Maine, the sea hammers ceaselessly, grinding rocks to smooth touchstones, the massive tides flooding, then deserting the countless miles of stony, mollusk-inhabited beaches. The saltwater meets the fresh a few yards from shore in the biological maternity ward called an estuary, and beyond that the bubbling stream cascades toward the sea from its parentage of a lake far inland.

In the South, a literal dribble flows downward until it meets oxygen-poor swamplands where a biologically defiant life propagates wildly. The swamp's waters find their way further southward and flow into the Gulf of Mexico whence pours the storied Rio Grande, which divides the United States and Mexico.

To the west, storm-ridden winds blow unkindly upon the steep cliffs and upon evergreens struggling for life among waterworn rocks. The Pacific is a gentle sea, but the continental shelf there is narrow, so deep water lies near the shore; and, like all women, the Pacific has her days. Some are tempestuous.

Heading eastward there is the Great Salt Lake and the reminder of prehistoric times when the land won a battle against the ancient seas. Still farther, there are the Great Lakes and beyond is Niagara Falls, a cascading torrent which has become almost a national symbol.

And among thousands of small, clear lakes in the Minnesota forest, in the heart of the country, a brook ripples its way through a maze of tree roots eventually joining with its brothers until it becomes a roaring river feeding life to the mighty Mississippi. Known to the Indians as "Great River," that giant slash of water drains one-third of the nation and is one of the greatest trade waterways in the world. Together with its chief tributary, the Missouri — called "Big Muddy" because of the vast amount of silt it carries — the Mississippi makes up one of the longest river systems in the world, about 3,986 miles. The Mississippi carried the rafts and boats of the early settlers and later the paddle-wheeled steamboats. Poets and novelists and song writers have made her famous. Mark Twain, who wrote *Life on the Mississippi,* is her most famous literary son, "Old Man River," her most famous musical accolade.

This is water, the vital fluid, the blood of civilization. With it we nourish crops, produce power, use it as a vehicle for transportation, farm it for food, play in it and utilize it for the industries of America. Water, fresh or saline, is wealth, and a great and new conservation movement has encompassed this rich resource so often abused in the past.

It is a mighty force which can be harnessed; the United States ranks first in the world in developed hydroelectric power. But when left to its own devices, this same water can wreak destruction or change the face of the land. The mile-deep Grand Canyon was etched by rushing water, and hurricane-spurred waves have ridden across valuable shore property leaving millions of dollars and grieving families behind to view the product of its power.

In northern Maine near the Canadian border a proposal to harness the extraordinarily high tides has been discussed for years, and should it materialize, electricity would be produced by their perpetual motion. Dams would connect to the land and islands, forming two huge tidal pools. The water rushing in at the beginning of high tide would turn generators, and at low tide the water would be released to turn them again.

River barges still ply the Mississippi carrying freight and passengers, as they have for nearly two centuries; ocean-going vessels can deliver cargo to the Midwest by traveling the St. Lawrence Seaway to the Great Lakes;

Coast at Monterey, California.

Seashells, Cape Hatteras, North Carolina.

Colorado River, Canyonlands National Park, Utah.

both oceans yield millions of tons of food a year—fish, crabs, oysters, clams, kelp—to feed a growing nation.

Water has given rise to many near-miracles, and perhaps the most miraculous of all is the bringing of it to where it is needed. The Romans accomplished this with aqueducts, and their basic design is the same as the engineering feat which carries water from Arizona hundreds of miles to the millions of inhabitants of Los Angeles.

Lake Mead in Nevada was a canyon a few years ago, then a dam was built to hold back the water for power generation. Page, Arizona, is a dusty town surrounded by a bleak land inhabited by Navajo Indians. A decade ago, Page was non-existent, then the U.S. Bureau of Reclamation began the damming of Glen Canyon, turning the lovely and desolate earth fracture into a massive lake which will stretch for 180 miles up the canyon when it is finally filled. Page grew around the dam site, and shortly became a bustling community catering to those Southwesterners flocking to this new recreational opportunity.

There are still remains of the system of canals which traversed much of the nation in the early 19th century. A few miles outside Boston can be found great stone blocks forming the banks of the old Middlesex Canal, a waterway used to ferry cargo from the industrial cities north to the great seaport. There are other vast canal systems scattered across the Northeast quarter of the nation, and the broad-shouldered men who laboriously pushed long poles into the mud below to propel their squat crafts did much to expand the then-budding country.

There is beauty in water, too, from the roar of the Yellowstone River lacing its way beneath rainbow-tinted mist to a canyon 300 feet below, to the craggy, cold grandeur of Lake Superior and the pristine splendor of Maine's Allagash River, surrounded by a wilderness inaccessible enough to protect its evergreen-lined banks and the shores of the lakes it connects.

Water is recreation. Any summer weekend in America, lakes and rivers are filled with fishermen and boating enthusiasts. The adventurers ride kayaks and rubber rafts down the torrents called the Snake and Colorado Rivers, pitting their skills against vicious currents and rocks hidden beneath the foamy fury. Airboats, a curious combination of airplane and shallow-draft boat, carry tourists, fishermen and trappers across the great swamps of the Southeast.

Water is the lifestream of the Everglades at the southern tip of Florida, for without it the wildlife in the great swamp would not exist. Spoonbills, herons and egrets nest in the greenery, and an occasional alligator is found sunning itself on a mossy rock. Scattered across the Everglades are hammocks crowded with budding trees and waterways filled with water hyacinths, a beautiful but troublesome weed which chokes navigation lanes and fishing areas.

A continent away lies a once-barren region, dust-ridden and sprinkled with cactus. Southeastern California, thanks to water, now supplies much of the produce used by American housewives in winter, the land made fertile and yielding by an incredible irrigation system. Water is costly here, for every drop is imported, but it and the climate combine to give American housewives fresh vegetables in the dreary days when snow is covering much of the nation's landscape.

Water helps make food, then yields it to fishermen. Seines (nets designed for fishing) on both coasts collect thrashing tuna, sometimes weighing hundreds of pounds each, and chugging trawlers harvest millions of pounds of the sea's bounty from picturesque fishing ports. In regions of high tides there are curious fences rising from the water which capture fish with little effort. The weirs' tips are beneath the water at high tide, and the unwitting fish which swim in are netted out when the water ebbs. This simple but ingenious method of gathering food has been known to this continent for hundreds of years. A few years ago in Boston when construction men were digging the foundation for a new office building a half-mile from the water, the shovels uncovered a chain of "pickled" sticks placed in the ground a few inches apart. Archeologists soon determined it was an ancient fish weir, built centuries ago by a tribe of Indians.

Contemporary Indians spear spawning salmon on the Columbia River in the Northwest using the same methods as they did when the white man first saw them. The white man learned from the Indians how to seek tasty crabs in small tidal pools and to ensnare the succulent lobster in simple traps, a method still used by the vast majority of these fishermen.

Periods of drought periodically sweep across the nation and prompted legislation in both Washington and state capitals. Rivers polluted by industrial wastes and used as open sewers because of their convenience are now slowly being turned into sparkling blue streams, and more bodies of water join this list each year.

And as the sweet waters begin to return, man is turning his eye toward the sea, the great frontier which covers almost three-quarters of the earth's surface. Man has learned more of space in a decade than he has of the oceans in centuries.

Oceanographic institutions on both coasts are expanding their staffs of researchers, seeking new ways to utilize this great and relatively untapped natural resource to man's advantage. Private institutions such as the Shedd Aquarium in Chicago are creating an interest in the sea, and great universities and foundations are joining their talents in unprecedented cooperation to study the mysteries of the oceans of the world.

Water is life, a joy of taste and sound and sight.

Prairies: The Sea of Grass

A few years ago the eminent naturalist and author, Donald Culross Peattie, was asked to write an article about the part of the American landscape he considered the most beautiful. His answer shocked many readers. The gently rolling country of Illinois was his answer. He said he felt that it was "beautiful as only a great fertile plain can be beautiful," and added that he never knew a place "where birdsong and frogs sounded so sweet." Millions of Midwesterners were not surprised at all.

The central United States spreads for mile after mile, ribbons of tar connecting great cities with tiny hamlets; gleaming white farms set back from the roads, surrounded by checkerboard fields of black, newly plowed earth or of growing green; acre after endless acre of wheat gleaming golden under the summer sun; spikes of corn swaying in the warm August breeze.

A farm here is not a scant few acres wrested from the forest with sweat and oxen, nor is it dry land with thin topsoil challenging all but weeds to grow. The earth is fertile and black with nutrients, washed for millenniums from the mountains and spread across the flat surfaces with a giant hand. Not all prairie land is so productive, but the plains and prairies of the United States supply much of the nation's food. Where the land is somewhat stony and remote, great herds of cattle graze on the luxuriant summer grasses.

Originally most of this land made up the famous Sea of Grass, the tall-grass prairies that stretched from Alberta to Texas and the Rockies to the Missouri-Mississippi Valleys. These magnificent grasslands — where grasses often grew as tall as men and billowed in the wind like the waves of the

(Continued on page 35)

Giant redwood, California.

Fallen crab apples, Illinois.

Autumn color. Vermont.

Lonely Horse Mill, Colorado.

Monument Valley, Arizona.

Devil's Playground, Mojave Desert, California.

Waterfalls, upstate New York.

Swamp trees, Kentucky.

Olympic Mountains, Washington.

sea — are now largely gone, their rich earth taken over by man for farming; comparatively little is left for the wild plants and animals some of which have moved to other habitats, such as the bison which went farther west. But today the old prairies retain something of their former character, and they have become America's breadbasket.

Today's prairies are somewhat different from the old, now gently easing into northern Ohio and Indiana and southern Michigan, where during the past century and a half forests have given way to man-made grasslands dotted with tiny groves of trees.

The climate throughout this vast area varies from dry and cold to hot and humid, and thus does the bounty of the land. Part of it is thinly forested, other sections are void of trees. Some of it is dry, some of it moist with the side flows from rivers draining beneath the rich land, releasing water to be lifted to the surface by the capillary action of roots.

At the headwaters of the Illinois and Wabash and south and west of Lake Michigan the land is smooth and flat, unlike the remainder which rolls and climbs in an undulating pattern broken with occasional streams. In depressions in the rolling prairie, the grasses grow as thick and tall as they did decades ago. Above, the greenery is thin, but all becomes a palette of colors in spring and summer when wildflowers sprout and paint the landscape with splatters of vivid reds and oranges and yellows.

These particular prairies (which are more precisely called parklands) have an annual average rainfall of from 20 to 35 inches. They form a separation belt between the forests and the short-grass Great Plains (more precisely called steppes) where rainfall averages 12 to 20 inches. Their 200 to 600 miles of width in a broad strip from north to south act as catalyst of sorts for the extremes on either side.

To the east, the climate and soil is paralleled by the forests, rich and wet. As the band spreads westward, rainfall lessens and the soil grows a bit less fertile, although it is often so productive that the expression "plain" belies the landscape.

Here and there are streams fringed with trees, and where there are wet valleys, there are long stretches of towering green. Often the wooded areas are only a few yards wide on either side of the running water; in other places the belt of trees is so broad it reaches from one stream to another, all sprouted from seeds carried by the winds from the forests.

Where trees are scarce, grasses cover the landscape: dropseed, wildlune, Muhlenberg, porcupine and wild rye. In places, hickory, elm, cottonwood, maple and ash have been slowly multiplying alongside these grasses since the end of the great fires which once raped the area.

The Indians often used to set the fires as protection against the white man. So great were these walls of flame that even rivers could not stop their greedy flight. The Platt and Boonville Rivers could not hold back the fires in 1835 when a massive blaze spread across the prairie. In 1871, another great fire crossed the Vermilion and James Rivers, reverting the land back half a decade.

Swathing wheat, South Dakota.

Indians touched fire to the wind-dried grasses to discourage the settlers who could not find forage for their horses and cattle after the fires retreated beyond the horizon. The fires negated much of the fertility of the land to the white man of the late 19th century, and the discouragement they faced was often monumental.

Small, controlled fires were often set around homes and growing fields, with the hope that the flames would stop and wither when they reached a place that could not furnish fuel. Cattlemen anxiously looked toward the skies when lightning bolts struck the earth, and when the inevitable fires grew closer they harnessed teams of horses to drag plows and create fireguards. Cowboys would team up to drag a piece of green rawhide along the line of fire.

The great XIT ranch almost caused its own undoing in 1885 when a weary cook for the cattle drovers accidentally set a small fire in the dried grass around his chuck wagon. The flames were out of control within

Oats, Pennsylvania.

minutes and burned the north end of the Texas Panhandle into Oklahoma's public land strip.

The devasting prairie fires were of greater peril than the Indians or cattle thieves. One fire in North Dakota burned for six weeks, and as late as 1947 a fire northwest of Pierre, South Dakota, ravaged more than 700 square miles in five counties.

For all its ferocities, the prairies offered much. The land was, and is, generous to its inhabitants. The top soil was deep, and when there were no trees settlers would build homes of chunks of sod, piling dried squares of deeply interlaced roots and earth one atop the other until they had an abode somewhat similar to the *hogan* of the Navajo.

The settler had game to hunt, deer and antelope and the once numerous prairie chicken, a relative of the ruffed grouse of the East. This spectacular bird is still to be found, and the male's unique dance and orchestration during the mating season is an unforgettable experience even for

37

the most traveled of hunters or bird watchers.

The stalking male bird puffs up the two air sacs on either side of his neck and booms a mighty sound from them while strutting along grassy knolls in competition with others of his sex, until finally he is chosen by a waiting hen. The spectacle of half a hundred birds noisily shouting their attributes and pounding the earth is indeed a delicious moment of the brief spring on the prairie.

Before the white man, and perhaps before the earliest of Indians, the prairie dog scampered across the ground to his community, its complexity matched in nature only by the bee. There are still whole "towns" of prairie dogs; tireless little creatures forever busy with their tunneling and food cropping.

This rodent is one of the sights of the prairie, a foot-long burrowing animal whose communities cover several acres and drop 10 to 12 feet below the surface. Man has encroached upon the wild and open spaces they preferred for their homes, and now they have been relegated to the uninhabited places. But their habits have not changed. The animals dig deep burrows for homes, enlarging them here and there for sleeping quarters. Unlike their cousins, the woodchucks of the East, they congregate by the hundreds, and move as a pack when the forage grows too thin to support life.

Like the prairie dog, man has moved on and his cultural instincts also drew him together in great cities. He is drawing his life from the land, but has learned that cultivating it and feeding it makes his life much richer, and he does not become a nomad, forever seeking the solitude of the desolate plain or the open prairie. He may move apart from his fellows as have many of Iowa's wheat farmers, but he has never turned his back on others. The prairies were never a place for man to relax. And, fortunately for America and the world, the people of this region have never relaxed, for without their efforts upon this beneficent land the abundance of America, the basis of her strength, would be lost.

Men to Match Mountains

Here was a man to hold against the world,
A man to match the mountains and the sea.

When in 1901 the American poet Edwin Markham wrote these lines about Abraham Lincoln — the man who made the nation finally a union — it was inevitable that he should compare Lincoln's strength with that great natural barrier, the surmounting of which, at the Continental Divide, essentially completed the westward expansion over the continent. Americans have always measured their heroes against the mightiest and the

Prairie dog, South Dakota.

Reflections, Sierra Nevada, California.

Canyon de Chelly National Monument, Arizona.

mountains of their land offered a supreme comparison.

Americans have been and remain hill-seekers, either to revel in the undulating greenery across a mountain chain or to climb one to see what lies beyond. Each peak they have sought has become at once a pinnacle of despair or triumph; a wind-sheltered haven for a terraced farm or a nightmare of roaring storm waters; a place of peace or savagery or triumph; and above all, solitude.

But man conquered the hills more often than he was defeated by them. Each rise in the ground was a new barrier to the settling of America and, to the men and women newly arrived from Europe, these hills called for adapting to a new way of life.

The Appalachians of the East were one of the first formidable barriers to face the settlers, but there was the Cherokee as well as the hills to battle. When the Indians were defeated in 1761, a tidal wave of emigrants moved into the Great Smokies. Many followed the path discovered more than a decade earlier when Dr. Thomas Walker, a Virginia physician, walked south and found the Cumberland Gap into Kentucky. At the same time the family

of Daniel Boone traveled to North Carolina. Eastern Kentucky and Tennessee became the home of English, Scots-Irish, Huguenots and Germans whose descendants lived in these mountains virtually undisturbed well into the 20th century.

The beauty of the Great Smoky Mountains and the plenitude of rich land, fish and game drew tens of thousands of settlers who found in the hills nearly all they needed for existence. Cedar, oak and chestnut were split to make shingles and fence rails. Nuts were gathered for foods and herbs were used for medicines. Cabins were built of logs laboriously felled with axes or fire, and chimneys were built of stone and native clay, or of woven twigs and clay where stone was scarce. Ashes from the massive fireplaces mixed with lye made soap, sheep grazing in green pastures yielded mutton and wool, and the gifts of the hills were almost infinite.

Beyond Appalachia lay a thousand miles of relatively flat land, then it began to rise in a new obstacle to those finding their way west — the Rockies. Unlike the Great Smoky Mountains or the rich but gentle hills and Green and White Mountains of New England, these were often forbidding. To surmount them was not easy and often impossible. Wind-broomed stretches of the Southwest held little food and less water; the heights of the Rockies, though lovely in the spring, were cold, and the icy peaks were a gigantic and sometimes impassable fence holding back explorers and their horses.

The first Europeans to use a Rocky Mountain pass were 22 members of a Spanish scouting party in 1540, the pass today called La Glorieta, at the southern tip of the Sangre de Cristo Mountains near Santa Fe. In the 1820's and 1830's that legendary breed of men, the Mountain Men, came to the Rockies. Competition for furs drove these men into unknown regions of the mountains and into a lonely, fierce life. James Bridger, Kit Carson, Jedediah Smith, the Sublette brothers, William and Milton — these men, singly or in small groups, staked out many of the first trails to Oregon and California, routes which have become the major highways of today.

In the later 19th century, migrants spread out from the Old Northwest Territory and Old South into Texas, and their tales of the land to the west drew still more settlers and attracted new families from across the Atlantic. California was drawn into the American orbit as Mexican rule of the Pacific grew weaker. Los Angeles, Monterey and San Diego were sparsely settled and dusty towns, but the attraction of new lands to explore caught the fancy of the young nation, and America was on the move across mountains again.

In the winter of 1846-1847, a band of emigrants who left Missouri encountered horrors in the mountains. The unrelenting Sierra Nevada mountains loosened a burst of snow in an early winter, trapping the Donner Party. Unable to retrace their steps, they built huts and prepared to wait out the storm at Truckee Lake.

The storms multiplied, and food ran out. In desperation the party boiled oxhides and bones, then turned to cannibalism. The horror of the

Columbia River, Crown Point, Oregon.

mountains and what it had done to their friends so repelled 15 members of the party that they fled and made their way to California. Volunteers scaled the mountains and brought the survivors to safety. Of the 87 persons stranded by the storm, the mountains left only 47 alive.

There were other epic battles of man against mountain, trappers lost or starved to death in the vast reaches; wagon trains of pioneers swept down stream beds swollen in minutes by flash floods; wagon axles snapped and the legs of horses and oxen broken by rolling boulders; avalanches obliterating a trail. Yet they moved on, inching their way across the mountains, telling epic tales in the formation of the United States.

As civilization pressed onward, new riches were discovered in California and in the mountains which soon became lined with destroyed wagons, bones and graves as emigrants followed the Oregon Trail or the Truckee River.

Towns grew overnight in the mountains — Virginia City in Nevada, Tombstone in Arizona, Denver in Colorado — to become lusty supply headquarters for the brawling prospectors. Some of the men, like the towns, made their fortunes, and others withered. The bones of ghost towns such as Bodie, California, are still there to see. The men have disappeared.

The dusty trails over the mountains were improved to become roads, and finally the railroad spanned the continent. The struggle with the mountains had passed its climax for young America, but even with the turn of the 20th century much remained to be explored in the mountains.

Americans are still discovering the mountains, east and west, by visiting the national parks which encompass many of the picturesque peaks. Paved roads pass over and through many of them, but the spirit of adventure is still alive for those who seek the hills on foot with civilization at their backs as did the pioneers two centuries ago.

The Great American Desert

On the way west, after the sea, after the forest, after the rivers and mountains — after these barriers, each a part of the American wilderness, came the desert and semidesert area frequently called the Great American Desert, one of the most awesome natural realms of the continent.

Shifting sands, skull-cracking heat and patches of alkali baked in the ceaseless sun form but a fraction of the characteristics of the Great American Desert. Indeed, the untiring efforts of man have created great cities in its apparent wastes and turned the cracked earth into massive farms. What is left may never be conquered by man, and its ruggedness and wild beauty will be left as a heritage for tomorrow's children.

The desert covers about a quarter of the United States, spreading in a great inverted "U" from Nevada through southern California — where the torrid wastelands of the Mojave Desert and Death Valley are located — to Baja California and east Texas. This desert area is surrounded by a great swath of scrublands or semidesert, which also runs in a narrow band along the eastern edge of the mountain barrier. The boundaries between desert and scrublands change with the rainfall, for water, or the lack of it, is the determination of a desert.

The Great American Desert is a land of extremes, for the region encompasses barren plateaus, dry stream beds, mountains and valleys covered with thin grass, cactus, sage, soapweed, yucca and rolling sand dunes where the noon sun is often unbearable and the nights bring freezing temperatures.

The contrasts are everywhere — forbidding Death Valley 270 feet below sea level and mountains nearly three miles high; barren plains bordered by mountains; dry lakes floored with salt; glittering blue bodies of water reflecting the summer clouds; mile after countless mile of dusty land punctuated with tumbleweed, sage and green cactus.

The Great American Desert is many things, and life has adapted to them. Remarkable plant life flourishes, the prickly pear with its delicious fruit, the barrel cactus and saguaro, all capable of glutting themselves on water, then using it sparingly to sustain life during dry seasons. Excessive transpiration is generally the last step toward doom for ordinary trees and plants, but those on the desert, the cactuses, withdraw themselves from the boiling sun within waxy skins to protect their broad surface from direct rays.

There are animals, such as certain desert rodents, which have perhaps never tasted a drop of free water. Many make their homes in burrows both for protection from the sun and predators.

Man has adapted to the desert, not by evolution but by ingenuity. Early Indians created symmetrical and colorful pottery from the native clays, then used them to water their crops of corn, melons and beans. They diverted trickling streams into ditches to irrigate their crops and formed harmonious and intricate cultures. Marvelous homes built into the sheer walls of cliffs are still there to see, mute testimony to the tenaciousness of these early peoples in conquering the land.

The white man — the Spaniards — came in the early 16th century, spurred on by reports of great cities. They explored much of the desert, looting and killing, but never finding their "El Dorado." The land, however, took its vengeance and accounted for the lives of many of the explorers.

Other explorers trekked across the land, the most famous of which were Lewis and Clark, while the trappers arrived to pit their endurance and skills against the land so that the gentry of the East and Europe might wear fur garments.

Missouri, for all practical purposes, was the western boundary of the United States then, and beyond it lay the greatest challenge young America then knew. The explorers were not grizzled trappers, gold-hungry miners or adventurous young men. They were families, thousands upon thousands of them, setting out to write the most prominent chapter in American history since the Revolutionary War.

They were told that beyond the desert lay rich land, a pleasant climate and a generous sun. So they set out, a months-long trip fraught with the

California condor, Los Padres National Forest, California.

Colorado Desert, southern California.

dangers of Indians, starvation, thirst, fever and the incomparable misery of wagon wheels or axles broken on jutting rocks or deep, sun-baked ruts.

Missionaries led the way, followed first by a Massachusetts merchant, Nathaniel J. Wyeth, who journied across the northern rim of the desert to the Northwest. A year later, in 1834, Wyeth again made the trip and paved the foundation for the Oregon Trail later used by thousands of emigrants. This perilous journey was generally made in a formation of "prairie schooners," ungainly looking but substantial wagons with bodies so tightly joined and caulked they could float across the many rivers barring their way to their promised land.

Silver was discovered in Nevada in 1858, and the Comstock Lode together with the earlier great California gold strike became a magnet causing adventurers to cross the Great American Desert, to seek their fortunes in the mountains or in the black sand at the bottom of a stream rather than in the fertile and virgin land which attracted the earlier pioneers.

In 1830, just two years before the great emigration began, an intense man named Joseph Smith labored with a great call. He drew a few believers around him in Fayette, New York, and founded the Mormon faith which was to have the most compelling effect on the Great American Desert in its history. Smith's Church of the Latter Day Saints drew converts from those inclined to believe and brickbats from the scorners.

Smith brought his band from the intolerance of New York to Ohio, then to Missouri and Illinois where he found more of the same, and the Mormons were forced to move again. Smith and his brother were murdered, and the harried people looked to Brigham Young for leadership.

Young gathered his martyred flock and followed an advance party westward, forced to move in winter because of prejudices and harassments they found in Illinois. In the spring of 1847, the advance guard moved out, leaving behind some 16,000 Mormons who were to follow later when bridges had been built and gardens planted for them by the party.

Onward they moved, carefully taking care of their own needs as well as those of the others who would follow. Finally they reached Utah. Young, who was stricken with fever, gazed across the panorma beneath Big Mountain, pointed with his finger from his bed in a wagon and said, "This is the place."

The Mormons claimed 210,000 square miles of land, all of Utah and Nevada and bits of the bordering states of California, Arizona, New Mexico, Wyoming, Oregon, Idaho and Colorado. Their claim was cut three years later, then again until finally it was agreed that the Mormons would own what is now the entire state of Utah—85,000 square miles.

They set to work, fortified by their newfound freedom from oppression and the shimmering waters of the Great Salt Lake. Water was life, and the Mormons put it to use, developing a great irrigation system from the mountain streams. Then in their mathematical exactness they plotted the streets and homesites of Salt Lake City.

Queen's Garden, Bryce Canyon National Park, Utah.

Lizard, Arizona.

47

That life was a struggle for the Mormons is at best an understatement. They fought drought, starvation and insects which destroyed their crops, yet worked together to create a vast city amidst the barren wastes until by 1865 they had 65,000 persons reaping the crops from more than 77,000 acres of irrigated land, a miracle of sorts which followed the early prophecy of the late Joseph Smith, the man who started it all.

The Great American Desert has always been a challenge, and the Indians who fought to retain their property were the greatest next to food and water. Stripping them of their rights was not perhaps the most illustrious chapter in American history, but to the pioneer it was survival of the fittest. The fittest and their cavalry armed with repeating rifles won, but it took decades to accomplish.

Great tribes of indignant redmen, most of their names now known to every school child, took up arms against the invaders, and made the words Navajo, Apache, Ute, Arapaho, Sioux, Comanche, Crow and Kiowa a curse to every traveler, rancher or farmer. The greatest battle of all was fought by a young and headstrong General George Custer whose soldiers were destroyed in action which led the cavalry to avenge the Little Big Horn in a bloody war which brought the Indians to their knees, but not until the 20th century was about to be born.

Tucked amidst such great events are the notes of the cattlemen, the stony-faced ranchers who at first gathered their herds from the wild cattle whose ancestors were the herd members turned loose by the Spanish settlers in the 16th and 17th centuries.

The abundant grass and water of the Great American Desert — it was there, for every desert has its oases — helped the men and their beasts to multiply until local demand died because of oversupply, and so the cattle drives were born.

A few thousand cattle made their way to Missouri and Louisiana, while others were driven across the desert to California to feed the gold-hunters. Little by little the cattle drives spread out until, by the 1870's, the long-horned Texas cattle found their way to Missouri where they were carried to Chicago by railroad.

The cattleman's enemy, the homesteader, hated even more than the livestock thieves or Indians, moved in and had a hard life of it. But life grew and flourished on the desert in spite of the hardships, until finally the lines were broken which once separated religion from religion, cattleman from farmer, Indian from white man. When peace came on the eve of the 20th century, there was only one war left — man against water, or the lack of it.

Prophecies, superstition and pseudoscientific nonsense made no inroads upon the Great American Desert; more water was needed but there was little. New farming techniques were tried, then used as gospel; rainmakers came and went, leaving little behind but broken promises and empty wallets; well drillers reaped fortunes for their labors.

Then the boldness of man bore fruit, and the desert followed the joy-

Ancient bristlecone pine, eastern California.

ous parade of the nation's bounty. Rain would not fall because of incantations, nor would artillery shells fired toward the heavens bring the needed moisture. Ingenuity would.

An aqueduct which took five years to build was completed in 1913, an engineering marvel crossing mountains and deserts to bring water more than 230 miles from the Owens River to Los Angeles, the growing city in Southern California whose artesian wells produced only brackish water.

The desert claimed new land for itself when the catastrophic drought of the mid-1930's created a vast area, including Oklahoma and parts of surrounding states, which became infamous as the "Dust Bowl." On the other hand, the U.S. Bureau of Reclamation, born in 1902, has literally carried life to the driest of the desert states. It created projects so mammoth they were decades beyond the thinking of the people of the day; it dammed gigantic rivers and diverted their waters through aqueducts and pipes to bring water to thirsty cities. In its wake it has left turmoil, mostly between conservationists and the dam builders.

Meanwhile, as the battle between a nation and its desert continues, the struggle has left neither the land nor the people quite as they were before. And where the desert remains in its primordial purity, its stark beauty perpetuates its own glory and challenge.

Seasons of the Land

Spring comes early to the estuary. The withered brown marsh grass gives way to sprouts of green pushing their heads above the high tide. One-celled animals and crustaceans, mollusks and insects generate offspring, and fishes move toward the wetlands to spawn so that their young can feed on the lesser creatures.

In New England, conifers shake the last of the snows from their branches and tiny streams form from the sun-prompted melt as warm breezes blow in from the south. Across the still-brown pastures woodchucks shake the last feelings of hibernation from their sleep-tousled bodies and strut from their deep dens in search of long-awaited breakfast. A doe, her belly heavy with fawn, noses through the thickening undergrowth hunting a safe and secluded place where she can give birth.

It is still winter on this April day in the North, but the promise of the season of awakening lies in the buds of dogwood and maple trees, growing thicker by the day until at once there is a bursting of green across the land.

In the mountains far to the west, southern winds pace across the ridges, taking with them the snow on lower meadows and swelling rivers with their water. Suddenly the grass is green and wild flowers cover the open places within days after the snow has disappeared.

The winter-wrinkled leaves on Pacific trees begin to green as the mysterious forces of nature gain a foothold and turn winter's dreariness aside.

Spring has arrived on the land, but it is only a debut of summer in another of the endless phases which maintain life, for weather is as vital to ecology as is each carefully chosen mineral, plant or animal. And nowhere are the four seasons as diverse and beautiful as in America.

Across the Great Plains, in the North and along the hillsides of New England there is a new sound on this eve of the summer: the plodding of horses' hoofs and the rumble of tractors plowing and harrowing the earth still black with spring-damp. Furrows lace the newly turned soil and seed is sown. The applegrowers of Oregon and Michigan finish their pruning, and California's vineyards are gently readied for the heavy harvest of

(Continued on page 55)

Spanish Peaks, southern Colorado.

Joshua Trees, California

Checkerboard farmlands, Kansas.

Niagara Falls, New York.

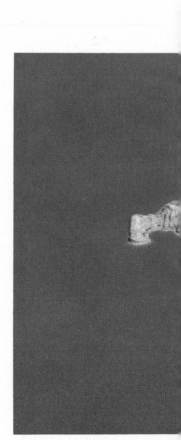

Door County, Wisconsin.

Grove of trees, Illinois.

Islands in Boysen Lake, Wyoming.

Craters of the Moon National Monument, Idaho.

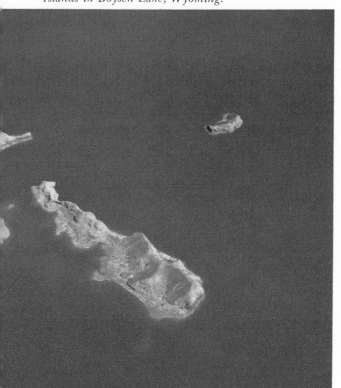

Western hemlock, Washington.

Badlands, South Dakota.

Coastline at sunset, California.

grapes only a few months away. Farmers in the dry Southwest have already started irrigating their crops which will be ready for harvest weeks ahead of native vegetables in the North and East.

The days grow warmer and wheat and rye and corn punctuate the soil with dots of green. The sparse leaves of oak and maple have unfolded and the season's first crop of hay is growing to maturity as the warm and indolent days of summer spread northward.

The striped bass have since returned to the sea and the white-tailed fawn is staggering on spindly legs. The woodchuck's young have dared venture beyond the earth-mound of their den, small fledgling sparrows have dropped to the ground here and there from their nests, and their mother swoops low to nudge the tiny bird, then in despair feeds it a wriggling earthworm.

Summer passes on, and in the fleeting days of warmth migrant workers bend over crops of beans and tomatoes as awkward-appearing threshing machines begin the long journey back and forth across fields of grain.

When September comes, the crops of the North have been harvested with barns and silos filled with baled hay and field corn. Huge packing houses near the vast field of vegetables are canning and freezing food for a nation. In the South where the climate changes but little, new crops of melons and lettuce and tomatoes are sown.

The first chill days of fall bring a change as sudden as those of spring. The rich green potato vines of Maine and the truck gardener's cucumbers shrivel and brown. Growth slows on the deciduous trees as the sap slows. Chemical changes turn the green handprints to fiery reds and yellows and oranges in the trees' last moment of glory before they are born again two seasons later. New England, Pennsylvania, New York, New Jersey and the upper Midwest are ablaze with color, while overhead, V's of snow geese migrate southward, their handsome narrow necks jutting ahead.

Still colder winds blow across the plains and the Dakota Badlands, and the cattle of the North Dakota rancher huddle together against the new sensation. The winter comes early to the Rockies and California's High Sierras. The high country of the West has settled in for its longest of all seasons, as a wind-spurred storm screams in from the north to laden the evergreens with a cloak of white and fill narrow passes with deep snow. Hundreds of miles to the south and east, 140-mile-long Death Valley now has temperatures more acceptable to man, after reaching well over 120 degrees in the summer, and tourists come in droves to enjoy the spectacle of the arrogantly beautiful gash between the mountains.

Winter has finally arrived in the mountains, but Florida still basks in comfortable temperatures. Suddenly, masses of tropical air meet in the Caribbean and a vortex of wind-fury is born far at sea. The hurricane feeds upon itself, growing larger, then veers to the northwest and aims for the palm-lined cities of Florida's east coast.

The hurricane strikes gently at first, its peripheral winds whipping beach sand and bending trees. Then the fury grows and the sea's waters increase until streets and bridges are covered with crashing, foam-tipped waves. Giant trees are uprooted and crash buildings. Expanses of plate glass shiver and break under the wind's hammer as wave after wave undermines buildings and scrapes away highway paving.

Then, as suddenly as it began, the winds cease and the tides are stilled. This is but the eye of the storm, the center of the whirling winds, and it is a dead calm. The storm is only half over, for the westward side of the hurricane has yet to hit in duplication of the initial destruction.

The storms to the north are not as immediately spectacular, but their destruction is as terrible, if slower. Drifting snows cover railroad tracks in the mountains, bury whole herds of cattle in the plains and fill highways

Frost pattern on window.

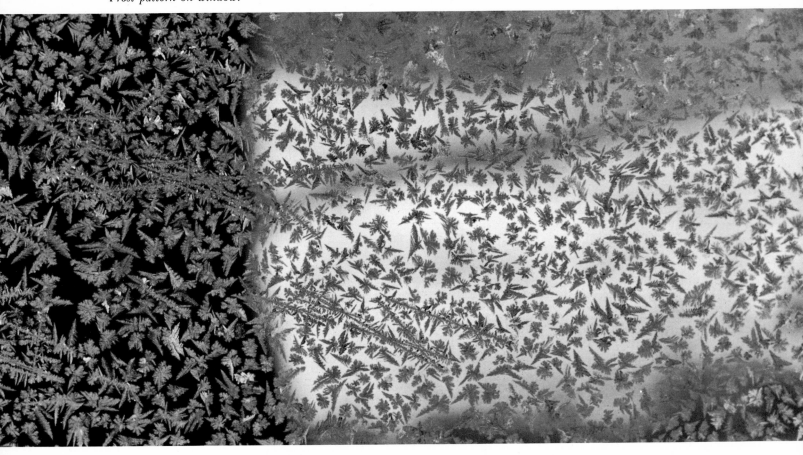

in the Northeast and Midwest, stranding motorists.

Each would trade "his weather" for another's, but each has its own furies. The tornadoes of northern Texas, Oklahoma, Kansas, Nebraska and southern Iowa have become part of a way of life, wreaking almost as much destruction as the hurricanes which threaten the East Coast.

Born of conflicting air currents and temperatures, these violent storms quickly form a huge funnel of darkness which spins like a top across the land, its low-pressure center literally sucking up houses, trees and barns after they have been loosened by the brief but violent winds at its outer edge. The hurricane can encompass hundreds of square miles, but an equal fury is contained at the tip of a tornado only a mile or two across. Its passage is brief, violent and destructive. Both hurricane and tornado are indicative of the size and temper of the American land.

It is January now, and the storm season is ended. Snow still falls in a wide stripe across the upper half of the nation, but it will soon abate. This month and the next sometimes bring the pleasant respite of a thaw, but winter will set in again with a bit less tenacity than it did before.

The snows are piled deeply, and tree branches sag beneath their weight. The sun is rising in the heavens and its rays grow warmer. Soon the evergreens will shake the last flakes from their needles and the ground will turn warm. The land, dried and cracked beneath the hot summer sun a half-year ago, will be moistened again as river beds slowly fill, then carry water downstream in the raging torrent which only spring can bring in this eternal change which takes place in a continual pattern. The four seasons are vibrant and full, as it should be in a dynamic nation made strong by contrasts and the might of man and his environment.

Nature as an Artist

The patient labors of the elements have been at work for millions of years, turning much of this treasured land into artistic creations in sand, stone and wood, each a unique and impressive formation.

Only time and the forces of wind and water could have created the Grand Canyon in Arizona or Natural Bridge in Virginia; only nature worked upon the outcroppings of granite in New England to shape green-patched mountains and a profile in stone bearing a remarkable likeness to an Indian sachem.

Water is perhaps the greatest force of all. Its constant seeking of lower levels and erosive force has carved such majestic places as the canyons of the West. Each drop of water falling in spring from an upland meadow carries with it perhaps only a particle of soil or sand. Multiply these by the billions of drops in a single day, and there is a rushing river carrying suspended bits of the earth, a liquid sandpaper of sorts working upon stone and loosening more bits until a few miles downstream the hand of the

Dinosaur National Monument, Utah and Colorado.

river bears a huge file, smoothing the stones in its path, freeing still more bits of stone and so on. Given enough time, a rushing river can wear a path a mile or more deep through solid rock.

The wind is just as tenacious. Gusts carry sand and topsoil, battering it against the sheer faces of cliffs until it, too, loosens more particles to become grit at its base, only to be hurled upward once more by the wind's force. Time again is the factor, for with enough of it the wind's power can sculpt dull-appearing mountains into exciting and surrealistic shapes, scrape away millenniums of geological formation in a few thousands of years to uncover colorful layer cakes of rock where once there was only a sandy and barren plateau.

In Utah, at the far end of Lake Powell formed by Glen Canyon Dam, lies the once nearly inaccessible Rainbow Bridge, the largest known natural bridge with a 278-foot span. This magnificent arch of red sandstone appears insignificant from the first opening in the foot trail, then its incredible height and breadth is suddenly evident when the visitor stands beneath and looks more than 300 feet up from the bed of the trickling creek which carved it. It is so enormous that it could fit over the Federal Capitol building.

This natural arch was formed by water rushing through the plateau, turning around high points of rock, then washing against them on the other side. Rainbow Bridge was one of these spurs in the way of the stream. It was hammered from both sides until the sandstone was finally pierced by the waters, then the stream found a new and shorter course, and the tiny hole was widened and rounded by the erosive action of the water. The wind took the final steps in this sculpture of nature, smoothing it and gentling the rough edges until it appeared as it does today, a monument to the work of nature's artistic hands.

Other exciting shapes, each unique, are found in Arches National Monument, also in Utah, where the shifting of the earth split an enormous layer of sandstone into orderly rows. Some have been leveled by the waters while nearly 90 others have been cut into the same shape as Rainbow Bridge.

A striking resemblance to extra-terrestrial terrain is seen at Craters of the Moon National Monument in Idaho. Here are 75 square miles of volcanic rock appearing like a view of the moon through a telescope. There are flat-topped cones of cooled lava looking like miniature but long-dead volcanoes and underground passageways formed when the upper surface cooled and the still-molten lava within drained away.

One of the most magnificent sights is Devils Tower in Wyoming where the mighty arm of nature is at once evident. The land is relatively flat, then abruptly there rises the tower, an 865-foot-high shaft of solid lava reaching for the sky.

The Badlands in South Dakota are aptly named, for before a modern highway reached it, the desolate region was a barren place but a geological wonder of unparalleled beauty. The evolution of the earth created layer upon layer of contrasting pastel hues, then the surface lifted. Wind-driven rains began to work upon alternating layers, baring their beauty in an endless variety of sub-strata.

*Timpanogos Cave National
Monument, Utah.*

All that nature has created is not on the surface. Giant caves are scattered across the nation, some of them so spectacular they defy description of their beauties. Carlsbad Caverns in New Mexico contains incredible formations of rock in chambers so large a church could be built without its spire touching the ceiling. The Big Room of Carlsbad has a side chamber reaching more than a third of a mile into the darkness, and its roof is more than 230 feet above the floor. Festoons of stalactites hang like opaque icicles from the ceilings in a variety of forms sometimes appearing like the mouth of a gigantic shark, an iceberg or the decorations of a baroque room.

To the east is Mammoth Cave, a natural wonder in Kentucky, which, unlike Carlsbad, is a series of long corridors rather than chambers. The hallways in the cellar of the earth connect massive dome-ceilinged rooms and deep pits. In ancient times, rivers flowed through these corridors when the land surface rose and the water seeped through cracks in the earth. Gradually the water ate away at the walls of its passageways, widening and deepening them into the majestic wonder seen today.

A few miles south of Salt Lake City on the north slope of snow-capped Mount Timpanogos in the Wasatch Mountains is Timpanogos Caves

Queen's Chamber, Carlsbad Caverns National Park, New Mexico.

Yentna Glacier, Alaska Range, southern Alaska.

National Monument, a series of three limestone caverns connected by man-made tunnels. Although Hansen Cave was discovered in 1887, the other two remained unknown until 1921. Slowly, dripstone is still being formed from tiny layers of limestone left on the tips of stalagmites by water drops that began untold centuries ago.

While water shapes jagged rock into weird, symmetrical forms and patterns, its action often serves merely to uncover what has already been created, such as the Badlands. It has also washed away the dust of the ages to uncover the remnants of an ancient forest in a part of northern Arizona so barren not even the tenacious sagebrush can gain a foothold.

The brilliant colors of the Petrified Forest are spread across the southern edge of Arizona's Painted Desert. Giant petrified logs are scattered across the landscape, tossed askew as if a devastating tornado had spent its fury on a forest, leveling massive trees in a helter-skelter pattern.

The wood has long since turned to stone, and the logs gleam under the desert sun, the jewel-like facets reflecting the rays. Nature spent 180-220 million years creating the Petrified Forest, beginning her labors when flood or storm felled living trees along the banks of a long-dead river. Little by little, the tree trunks were washed downstream and buried beneath layers of deep mud. Sediment from the rivers continued to cover the trees, and minerals permeated the logs to fill their cells. Quartz accumulated and replaced the wood to preserve it, and in doing so, duplicated every minute detail of it so that when the tree trunks finally rotted and disappeared, they were still present in the form of stone. Other minerals in the rivers' waters were carried by the ages to the wood, giving the brilliant colors seen today.

Not far away from Petrified Forest, in the northeast corner of Arizona, is Monument Valley, a majestic region where huge red sandstone pillared monoliths, arches, sand dunes and red earth are matched in pristine purity by a cloudless blue sky.

Water in the form of ice also is molder of the face of America. There are several glaciers in the northwestern United States but Alaska is the state of glaciers. Glacier Bay contains several and others such as the Mendenhall Glacier are nearby. Few, however, can match the great Yentna Glacier as it cuts through the rugged 600-mile-long Alaska Range, which also contains a number of famous peaks including 20,320-foot-high Mount McKinley, the highest in North America.

The joy of these wonders of nature is unparalleled but there is an equal satisfaction in them and others for every American. Most of these are protected by the Federal Government either as a national park or a national monument. They can never be exploited, razed, become housing developments or shoddy attractions. Each is testimony to a far-sighted nation that, while even in the throes of its period of the most rapid growth, paused to reflect upon its beauty then decreed this much, at least, would be left for tomorrow's children.

The National Park System began in 1872, when, after a two-year struggle, Judge Cornelius Hedges of Montana convinced Congress that the beautiful region of steaming geysers and bubbling springs in the terri-

Coral, Buck Island Reef National Monument, Virgin Islands.

Salt formations, Mono Lake, eastern California.

tory of Wyoming ought to be preserved. Yellowstone National Park was established that year, the first one in the world, and the action touched off a chain of similar parks which are still being created today in the United States and in others lands as far away as Japan.

The National Park Service was formed in 1916 to become part of the U. S. Department of the Interior. This division is responsible for some 25 million acres of land.

The newest national park is Canyonlands, established in 1964 in southeastern Utah, where the Green and Colorado Rivers converge. A craggy land of variety — arches, canyons, high plateaus, gorges, pillars and grabens — Canyonlands is, at present, for only the hardy. On the winding Colorado River, there are 27 miles of white water rapids through Cataract Canyon waiting to be traversed by experienced boatmen in rubber rafts or pontoons. Others see this untouched wilderness from airplanes or helicopters or from rough, narrow roads that lead into the park.

The first national monuments were decreed in 1906 by President Theodore Roosevelt who was so impressed with the Indian ruins of the Southwest he proclaimed that they be preserved. While the national parks are usually larger in scope than the monuments, the largest holding in the entire system is Katmai National Monument, a 2.7 million-acre site in Alaska. Parks are generally chosen for scenery, such as Yosemite in California or Olympic in Washington, while monuments have been created for singular beauty or uniqueness—such as the colorful coral formations of Buck Island Reef in the Virgin Islands, considered one of the outstanding marine gardens of the Caribbean, or the living wonders of the redwoods in Muir Woods National Monument in California.

None of the national monuments are more exceptional than Organ Pipe Cactus National Monument, along the Mexican border in southern Arizona. Part of the Sonora Desert, it has some 30 species of cactus but the most outstanding is the organpipe, the second largest cactus in the United States. One plant may have over 30 unbranched stems, sometimes reaching 20 feet in height. The monument includes a variety of habitats which account for the large number of animal species there, including the unusual desert pupfish which inhabits a spring-fed pond at Quitobaquito. Dinosaur National Monument on the Utah-Colorado border is also extraordinary—a combination of the world's most remarkable dinosaur fossil deposit and an exciting wilderness of canyons and ridges.

The states have also brought areas of unusual natural beauty under government protection, such as Indiana's sand dunes at the southern end of Lake Michigan and the Palisades, which are located along the western side of the Hudson River near its mouth. The Palisades, one of the finest natural sights in the Eastern part of the country, are included in an interstate park jointly established by New Jersey and New York. These cliffs of columnar lava are about 100 feet high at the southern end but increase to a striking 250-foot height about 15 miles away on the northern part of the ridge.

There are still regions in America not under the Federal system or

Wild mustangs, southern Montana.

protected by one of the states which are unspoiled and available to everyone. The rugged Allagash country of northern Maine beckons thousands of wilderness campers a year, and the massive Appalachian Trail spreads southward from Maine to Georgia, an easy foot trail following the great mountain ridge along America's East Coast. There are sparkling lakes in Minnesota, patches of colorful desert a few miles from the largest cities in Texas, sinewy cacti in bloom outside Phoenix, Arizona, rushing streams and cool forests only a short drive from Boston, Washington, Chicago, San Francisco and Minneapolis. It is the outdoors being discovered daily by more and more Americans seeking a respite from 20th century living and a handhold with the untouched land of yesteryear.

Americans Still Take to the Wilderness

Seasons matter little to Americans who love the outdoors, for each moment of the year is a cherished time to a camper, hunter, fisherman or hiker somewhere in this treasured land—people who revere their surroundings with the restless urge which seem to lie within each of us. The wilderness which once had been unavoidable to Americans has now become their necessary pleasure.

Millions of dollars are spent each year just for licenses by hunters and fishermen, and the burgeoning industry whose focal point is camping is a phenomenon one could find only here where the comforts of urban and suburban living may wane at anytime of the year and some unexplored place beyond calls for discovery.

America seems to be, somehow, in a joyous reversal of the progress which has marked every day of its growth since the 17th century. A simple vacation someplace away from home or a weekend journey to another city has been replaced by expeditions to national parks, a bold adventure hiking the hills or a week or two aboard a boat exploring exciting rivers like the Mississippi or secluded coves in the vast lakes scattered across the nation.

Hunting, once a basic element of survival, has become one of the most popular sports. Fishermen think little of traveling across half a continent to pursue a salmon, trout, tuna or tarpon.

Hundreds of thousands of campers annually pack their belongings for a week or two in the woods, leaving behind the luxuries of urban living. The New York construction worker, Chicago banker or San Francisco taxi driver finds a few days to hunt amidst the soaring flights of ducks in the Pacific flyway, deer in the Southwest, pheasant in the East or quail in the South. If all the hours Americans spent fighting big gamefish—blues, tarpon, tuna, swordfish and marlin—were added together, they would in a year's time literally equal centuries.

Wildlife in the United States has undergone a nearly complete reversal from half a century ago. Wise management and a growing awareness of conservation has brought back much of the game for the sportsmen and those who simply enjoy the presence of wildlife.

A striking example lies in the once nearly extinct bison, the American buffalo, that lumbering beast hunted to near-destruction less than a century ago. Protection and habitat improvement have brought the bison back from a few hundred animals to enormous herds grazing across the Great Plains. Wapiti, or American elk, were once also threatened with extinction, and now their migration a few days ahead of the snowstorms draws thousands of awed spectators each fall to Jackson, Wyoming. It is a memorable sight to see the spectacle of herds of elk moving down the Snake River valley toward the National Elk Refuge at Jackson, striding almost shoulder to shoulder through fields and down highways and quiet streets.

Other nearly extinct species have been granted a reprieve from destruction through stringent administration of fish and game laws. There are places where herds of shaggy wild mustangs still roam Montana and the Southwest, free and unendangered. A sighting of the huge and scarce California condor is always encouraging. The return each year of the rare whooping crane to a coastal wildlife refuge in Texas is viewed as an annual event by many who anxiously await the latest count on the number of birds, usually less than half a hundred. In the Northwest, the return of the salmon to rushing rivers to spawn is an attraction for still more thousands, and the migration of striped bass a whole continent to the east is a lure for thousands of fishermen.

The first brush of cold in the North signals literally millions of ducks

Bald eagle, national bird of the United States.

and geese to begin their migration to the South. Thanks to the efforts of conservation groups such as Ducks Unlimited both in the United States and Canada, breeding grounds have been protected and habitat improved to create a greater yield of waterfowl. A yearly survey by the United States sets hunting dates to harvest only a small percentage of ducks and geese.

Fish and game departments across the nation are continually battling pollution, reclaiming streams and ponds and pouring millions of pounds of hatchery-raised fish into these waters. Wildlife habitat is being improved by state organizations and literally thousands of private groups. Shrubs and trees providing food and cover for gamebirds are being planted and deer yards created to insure survival of whitetails over the rugged winters in the North. Huge tracts of land have been set side as public hunting grounds, which are enjoyed year-round by millions of hikers, picnickers, bird watchers and berry pickers.

Ardent preservationists are not always appreciative of hunting, but once the ideal conditions have been created by farmers and conservationists across the nation, the result is often such massive numbers of birds and game that a certain amount of this unique crop must be harvested so that a habitat will be left for their fellows.

Americans have always loved their land and the creatures which live on it, but today this love has become an admirable obsession with no climax in sight. The outdoors has become the focal point for an enormous industry.

Conservation is more than a topic in schools, it is a subject taught in many so that tomorrow's children might grow with an appreciation of their surroundings. Zoos with native species exist in every major city, and aquariums have become an important Sunday visit for many urban dwellers.

And in suburbia, where perhaps just a few years ago deer browsed and grouse or quail fed, in what is now the green backyard of an American family, there is usually nailed to a tree or post a mute symbol of their love for nature's creatures. It is a birdhouse.

Mount Rainier National Park, Washington.

69

A Nation
II | Conscious of its
Heritage

Legends, Explorers and Colonists

The chronicle of the United States of America is brief as histories go, but the intensity with which it has been lived and the awe in which it is held has given the American past a position as a source of strength that is virtually unparalleled in the life of nations. What began as a contest with a wilderness, a confrontation between man and nature, has become a legend and a heritage.

The vast reaches of coastline, washed by two oceans, the forests, the mountains, the plains, the prairies, the rivers and lakes are the elements that have challenged Americans ever since they first learned of the existence of this continent. In answering that challenge, people from all parts of the world have come to explore, to conquer, to conserve and to build.

When men first came is a question that has not been fully answered, and there are many theories. All scholars now agree that men were in America many thousands of years ago and it is believed that the first ones crossed from Asia in the region of the Bering Sea and made their way as far south as Patagonia at the southern extremity of South America.

The evidence of their existence is slight. Where they came from and where they went constitute academic problems that have kept scholars busy through decades, even centuries.

It would be difficult to say that America's heritage starts at any particular point in time. The Italian says in the late 15th century with Columbus.

*Heads of Washington, Jefferson, Theodore Roosevelt, Lincoln
carved into Mount Rushmore, South Dakota.*

The Spaniard says it began with the men who followed Columbus and went into Florida and up the Mississippi. The Scandinavians point to Leif Ericson in the 11th century; the Irish to St. Brendan sometime before the Vikings. The English speak of John Cabot and the French of Cartier.

The surest way to start a controversy among the various ethnic communities of the nation is to develop new evidence pointing to the arrival of any one before all others. On October 11, 1965, the vast Italian community was stunned when a group of scholars disclosed that the Norsemen had been in America centuries before Columbus. Had the announcement been made on any other day it would have passed with less controversy. Coming on the eve of Columbus Day, however, the announcement of a new piece of evidence regarding the early days of discovery caused an uproar. It was much like telling the Irish on the eve of St. Patrick's Day that St. Brendan was not the first to set foot on this soil.

Did St. Brendan ever reach America? Some scholars are certain that he did during his long voyages in the sixth century. There are stone remains in North Salem, New Hampshire, which show a connection with the architecture of monks' cells on islands off the coast of Ireland.

The Vinland map and the "Navigatio Sancti Brendani" are but part of the tradition of voyages to this continent in the early Christian era. Many others came and went according to the scraps of information now available. It has been said that Columbus knew of some of these voyages before he set out from Spain in 1492. Most historians reject the idea that Columbus visited Galway, Ireland, in 1490 to have a look at the manuscripts of St. Brendan.

However, it is doubtful if these scholars ever sat in a Galway pub at the side of Eyre Square on a November night when the rain was slashing against the windows and listened to an old man tell the story.

There, the *seanchai* will try to convince you that Columbus attended Mass in St. Nicholas Cathedral and then went over the records of Brendan's voyages. He might even confide that it was a Galwayman, Rice deCulvey, who went with Columbus as navigator of the *Santa Maria*.

A legend? Perhaps. But it, like the other stories of discovery, is part of the heritage of America.

Historians may scrutinize ancient ruins, water-soaked manuscripts and other fragmentary evidence—but there is more to it than the hard facts of evidence. The ethnic groups involved have a personal interest in the legends; they want to be known as part of the people who took part in the founding, the first development of a land which became the home of their family, perhaps only a generation ago.

With all due respect to the other claims, the honor still rests with Christopher Columbus. But even he did not know what he had found. He allegedly set out to prove that the world is round and to reach the Indies, and he thought that he had accomplished both objectives when he came ashore in the West Indies.

His voyages to the New World were disappointing to the people who had sponsored him. They were waiting for the great treasures of gold and

Coastal inlet and islands, Maine.

Castillo de San Marcos, St. Augustine, Florida.

silks from Cathay. None of these were found on the desiccated Bahamas or the other areas touched by Columbus.

The discoveries of Columbus were duly noted by envoys of the European nations stationed in Madrid, but they stirred no great enthusiasm. The English, however, outfitted another Genoese, John Cabot, and he made several voyages to the northern reaches of the continent.

None of the explorers who poked in and out of bays and rivers along the east coast of North America for nearly a century had the vaguest notion of the formidable barrier that stood between them and the Orient. The French penetrated the St. Lawrence River as far as the rapids and, in their excitement, named them Lachine—believing that beyond lay the fabulously rich lands of China and India.

The Spaniards, the conquistadores, operating with boldness and ruthlessness in Central and South America had more luck in finding the highly developed cultures of the Aztecs in Mexico and the Incas in South America. In 1519 Cortés led an expedition through the jungles of Yucatan and discovered the great wealth of Montezuma on the uplands of Mexico beyond. Some years later Pizarro moved into Peru and there found another highly developed culture. Other Spanish explorers penetrated the heart of the northern continent, moving up the Mississippi and making tentative forays into what is now California, the Southwest and north as far as Canada. For the most part these adventurous bands were seeking one thing—gold. Another motivation for exploration was based on the fact that, although Marco Polo had plotted a passageway to the land of spices and silks, the constant warfare along the caravan routes to the East made that road a precarious venture. A safer route was needed.

Some trading posts were set up along the east coast among the inlets of Maine. Daring fishermen from parts of northern Europe in the latter decades of the 16th century set up stations on the famous rockbound coast. These were temporary habitations; a place where they could come ashore and replenish their fresh water supply and stretch their legs before the long voyage home after a summer of fishing off the New England coast. The fisherman has endured and those who still work these waters are the descendants of a noble breed.

The tentative probings along the Atlantic coast—always with the dream that a passage could be found to the supposed treasure lands of the Orient—continued for many decades. The unfulfilled dreams of adventurous souls continued bright as the Spaniards in the 16th century uncovered the treasures of Mexico and Peru.

It remained for political and economic factors in England, however, to drive men toward thoughts of settling the area from Virginia northward to Maine. There was some idealism involved, but the men who financed the settlements were interested in the profits to be realized. The idealism was with those who participated.

At the time of Queen Elizabeth I the efficiency of a government depended on the amount of gold and precious metals in the royal coffers, or at least within the reach of the long arm of the tax collector. The amount of gold in turn depended on trade—but England's position in those days was not unlike that of today in some ways; she was importing more and more and exporting very little.

Fish came from the Dutch and other products from the Portuguese. England was growing more and more dependent on potential rivals for the necessities of life. At the same time her own products were having a more and more difficult time finding a market. Even when the markets were found English merchants were being persecuted in foreign cities.

When the English first considered the establishment of colonies in America two courses lay open to them. The knights of the realm, anxious to carve out new demesnes, favored the handing out of proprietary feudal grants. The merchants, looking toward profits, wanted chartered trading companies.

The first attempts to establish colonies in America were based on patents in the form of feudal tenure. The most famous of these was the attempt of Sir Walter Raleigh to place an enclave at Roanoke. The colony disappeared without a trace and Raleigh lost his fortune in the venture.

The lessons of the first attempts at colonization were not lost on the knights and merchants of England. The proprietary feudal grant continued to play a role in the settling of America, but England's moneymen saw to it that the chartered company, being more likely to succeed, was given preference.

The East India Company of England was chartered in 1600 for trade with established areas in the Indian Ocean. This organization, one of the most fabulous in history, was returning its investors 100 per cent profit within a decade. Its success led knights and merchants to turn their gaze on the wilderness of America where they saw glowing opportunities for new trade and development.

In 1606 King James I licensed a group of his subjects to "deduce and conduct two several colonies or plantations in America." The patents were given to two companies, the London Company, so-called because most of its members came from London, and the Plymouth Company, made up of merchants from Plymouth and the west of England.

On May 13, 1607, three small English ships drew near Jamestown Island in Virginia and moored to trees on shore. The next day, wrote George Percy, one of the party, "we landed all our men, which were set to work about the fortification, some to watch and ward as it was convenient. . . ." By mid-June, their fort had been finished and their grain planted. Thus was established the London Company's most famous colony at Jamestown, Virginia. Although the area was better suited as a start than the more forbidding New England area with its long cold winters, the men of Jamestown had a difficult struggle.

Names familiar to history fill the pages devoted to the story of Jamestown, but one stands out above all the rest—the redoubtable Captain John Smith.

Adventurer, explorer, historian and soldier-of-fortune, Smith was born in Lincolnshire in 1580. At an early age he ran away from home and saw service in the fighting in the Low Countries. At the opening of the 17th century he was fighting the Turks in Hungary, was captured and made a slave. He remained in servitude only a short time. He was back in England late in 1605 and immediately became interested in the explorations going on in America. He planned to join a Captain Charles Leigh who had set up a colony in what is now French Guiana. Before he could make arrangements word came back to London that the entire colony had been massacred. At the same time he was also interested in the explorations of Bartholomew Gosnold who had set up a temporary station at Cuttyhunk Island off Cape Cod in 1602.

Smith finally threw his lot in with the colonists headed for Virginia. He was not at that time one of the leaders of the adventure. Such an undertaking was very expensive and all the intrigues and politicking of that day were involved before the charter was granted by his "gracious" majesty.

The sturdy adventurer was named to the resident council which would run the colony in Virginia under orders from the Royal Council in London. Before the small fleet even reached the shores of America, however, Smith was in trouble. He was charged with mutiny and imprisoned. But when the three ships reached Cape Henry the ceremonious opening of a sealed box containing the names of the council members revealed that Smith was one of them.

In the months that followed, it was Smith who kept the colony building and trading. It was also he who took parties north and south and deep into the forests, along tree-shaded rivers to meet the Indians. Despite his efforts conditions in the colony went from bad to worse.

In 1609 the London Company, worried about its investment, sent out Sir Thomas Gates as "sole and absolute Governor," with 500 settlers in nine ships. Two of the ships were wrecked and only half the new settlers arrived alive. Gates took one look at the 67 starving men scattered along the James River and decided to abandon the colony.

Here the hand of fate took over. As he was sailing down the bay with the survivors he met Lord De La Warr coming with new recruits and supplies. De La Warr convinced Gates to turn back and thus saved the colony.

When one mentions Captain John Smith the immediate thought is "Pocahontas." It is on the Indian maiden's plea for Smith's life that most of his fame lies—yet it is a very small part of his life in North America. In fact, many historians dispute the authenticity of the incident, claiming that it was a hoax and refusing to believe most of what Smith later wrote about his adventures in this country. Some story-tellers have tried to make a romance out of the incident. This seems hardly likely since Pocahontas, who later married Englishman John Rolfe, was a child of 12 at the time and Smith was hardly a matinee idol.

The doubts are cast because Smith did not mention the incident in his first reports on his activities in Virginia. The story is first told in his *Generall Historie of Virginia,* published in 1624. The question is asked

Making pottery, Jamestown, Virginia.

Jamestown ship replicas, Hampton Roads, Virginia.

Mayflower II, *Plymouth Harbor, Massachusetts.*

as to why he did not tell it before. Perhaps the soldier-explorer did not want people to know that his life depended on a half-naked Indian child, particularly while he was still in the colony. In any case it is strange that the fame of the man who did so much to establish the first English colony on these shores should have to depend on 10 lines in a 248-page volume for his niche in history.

New England and New Amsterdam

Economics and religion combined during the establishment of the first colonies in America. In Virginia it was purely economics. In the founding of the Plymouth Colony it was a combination of the two.

The Pilgrims, or Separatists as they were known in England, left their homeland in 1608 in search of religious freedom. Holland at that time was their first choice and they settled in Leyden. The university city accepted the wandering band, but without any overwhelming enthusiasm. The Pilgrims soon found many reasons for dissatisfaction. Work was difficult to find and most of the men were artisans—William Bradford was a weaver, Robert Cushman was a wool comber, Isaac Allerton was a tailor. There were also carpenters, cabinetmakers, watchmakers and makers of smoking pipes among the group, but only a handful with business experience. Then, too, they found their children were picking up the Dutch language and forgetting the customs and conventions of England.

The discontented religious band started to look at the various prospects. Many of the merchant companies doing business in America had produced brochures for the purpose of interesting investors in their projects. History could have been very different if the Pilgrim leaders had listened to the salesmen of the Dutch West India Company who were anxious to find new settlers for their holdings in the Caribbean. A number of decisions had to be made and they were difficult. Virginia was English, but it was Anglican, which could lead to trouble; the climate of the Dutch colonies did not sound too healthy.

About this time Thomas Weston, an English merchant doing business in the Low Countries, arrived on the scene and convinced the congregation that a group of his associates in London could provide the needed capital for a colony in the New World. A joint-stock company was set up. Each person over 16 going to the colony was rated £10 sterling and this was considered a single share. Those who stayed home and contributed only money also had shares at the same rate. The joint-stock venture was to continue for seven years during which time all profits from "trade, traffic, trucking, working, fishing, or any other means" would remain in the common stock.

Like many a promoter, Weston turned out to be better at promising than producing. After months of "clamors and jangling" the Pilgrims were able to obtain two ships, the 180-ton *Mayflower,* the most famous ship in American history, and the 60-ton *Speedwell.* The financial disarray is evident from a report that before the ships left port the Pilgrims had to sell £60 worth of butter to pay off a £100 debt.

The *Speedwell* proved unseaworthy and was abandoned at Plymouth, England. This discouraged a number of the Pilgrims, but those remaining all crowded onto the *Mayflower*.

Landfall in the New World, after three months afloat was made at Provincetown, on the tip of Cape Cod, a windswept area of sand dunes— and a most inhospitable place in late November.

The Pilgrims had expected to land farther south, around the entrance to the Hudson River, but after the long tedious voyage any land looked good to them. A shallop was sent out and made some explorations along the

Plimoth Plantation,
Plymouth, Massachusetts.

coast as far north as Plymouth where a fair harbor was found. The *Mayflower* pulled in there and according to tradition they stepped ashore on the enshrined boulder now known as Plymouth Rock. The 102 people aboard the ship were willing to settle down on any dry land. They little knew the troubles that faced them; the disease, the lack of food, the problems of health.

Almost everyone knows the story of Myles Standish (whom the Pilgrims hired as their military leader) , Priscilla Mullin and John Alden, but neither they nor anyone else could have lived in the barren New England winter had it not been for several friendly Indians. Squanto and Massasoit came to help; to show the woebegone, but hopeful, Pilgrims how to plant and raise food.

Here again we find that people arriving on American shores probably had help from those who preceded them. Squanto may have talked with some earlier visitors, the fishermen or the Jesuits, and it is reported that he had even visited England.

Once ashore at Plymouth the Pilgrims found their troubles had only begun. The winter was severe, supplies were inadequate and disease struck down many of the settlers. Added to this was the hard, cold economic fact that when the *Mayflower* set sail for home in the spring of 1621 she had nothing in her hold to cheer the merchants in London who had put up money for the venture.

Harsh notes started back and forth across the ocean and the financial problems of the little colony went from bad to worse. Not only were there controversies among the leaders in Plymouth, but the backers in London started to quarrel among themselves.

In 1623 a small pinnace named the *Little James* was sent to the colony. It was intended that the vessel would help the colonists with their fishing and trading. The ship had been commissioned to allow her to capture prize vessels and when the captain failed to capture a passing French craft the crew became "rude."

Governor William Bradford found himself faced with the first maritime strike in American history. The crew wanted no part of fishing and trading; there was more money in privateering. The Governor had to negotiate a wage agreement and the pinnace set off for Narragansett country but came back empty handed; the Dutch outtraded them at every turn. Later the *Little James* lost a mast and she sank off the coast of Maine. It cost £500 to raise her and she returned to England where one of the merchant company had her seized in payment for a debt owed to him by others of the company.

This was only one of the many calamitous incidents that plagued the colony as it struggled to maintain a foothold in the New World. But the little band continued to struggle against almost insurmountable problems.

Today the *Mayflower II,* a replica of the original vessel, is berthed in Plymouth Harbor. Several miles south Plimoth Plantation has been re-created on a slope overlooking the wide expanse of Massachusetts Bay. On a pleasant summer day one can wander down the street and visit the homes of Governor William Bradford, Priscilla Mullins and many of the others. The herb gardens have been duplicated, the sawmill where shingles were made, the fort, from which a shot was never fired in anger, all have been recreated after painstaking research. It was here, according to tradition that Thanksgiving Day was originated. After the first harvest the Pilgrims invited their Indian friends in for a feast to offer prayerful thanks to God for having been bountiful.

These people prevailed over misfortune, as did the millions who were to follow them to these shores. They were deeply religious, but certainly not of the meditative or cloistered order. They were hard workers who carved out one of the first niches of what has become the most affluent nation in the world.

While the Pilgrims were striving to pay off their "debts hopeful and desperate," another group seeking religious freedom arrived on the shore of America. These were the Puritans.

Like the colonists of Jamestown and Plymouth and other less successful settlers, they received a royal patent allowing them to move into a section

Windmill, Cape Cod, Massachusetts.

of the New World. However, they startled the London officials by announcing that the backers of the project were among the men planning to cross the ocean. In previous adventures the backers had remained in England to protect the interests of the investors. Governor John Winthrop and his stern-visaged company, however, changed all that.

They came with adequate provisions and full backing. Whether or not they had heard about the misadventures of their neighbors in Plymouth is not recorded. But it is certain they made none of the mistakes which almost spelled disaster on the South Shore.

The Pilgrims sought religious freedom and as far as is known they were willing to extend it to others. Not so the Puritans.

The Puritans set up a theocratic state in Boston and Salem and gave short shrift to anybody who disagreed with them. During the 17th century and well into the 18th, many dissenters were to feel the wrath of the self-righteous leaders of the Massachusetts Bay Colony.

One of the most famous of the dissenters was Anne Hutchinson who came to the colony shortly after her pastor, the Rev. John Cotton, announced that he was headed for the New World. Mrs. Hutchinson persuaded her husband, William, to make the trip—possibly so that she could continue to argue about the Bible with her favorite minister.

Anne believed in the covenant of grace; that is, that the spiritual state of holiness does not depend on good works. It so happened that the Puritans of Massachusetts Bay believed otherwise and Anne was banished from the colony in 1637. She and her husband moved to Newport, Rhode Island, and after his death she went to New York, somewhere in the Westchester County area. She befriended the Indians in the area, but they attacked her home and killed her.

Roger Williams, a Salem minister, aroused the ire of Governor Winthrop with radical ideas in favor of religious liberty. He was eventually forced to flee the colony to avoid arrest. He later founded the Rhode Island colony.

Connecticut was founded in 1636 by the Rev. Thomas Hooker and a group of his followers. They left Massachusetts without being banished. In 1639 the freeholders or voters met in convention and formulated a paper called Fundamental Orders. It set up rules and regulations for the colony which was operating without a charter and is considered the first constitution ever devised in America.

Antique hunter's decoys, Massachusetts.

While the English were setting up colonies in Virginia and in New England the Dutch were taking over the area on both sides of the Hudson River. Their system of colonization differed from the other groups in a number of ways after the Dutch West Indies Company found it difficult to get people to move across the ocean.

At about the same time the Puritans moved into Massachusetts, the Dutch issued a charter which allowed large land grants and the title of "patroon" to those who brought 50 or more persons into the colony for a period of four years or more. The system flourished for a time, but then the English became conscious of the fact that this Dutch Hudson River line cut off the colonies in the north from those in the south.

King Charles II in 1664 granted the area of New Amsterdam to his brother, the Duke of York. The Duke stayed at home but he sent an expedition over to take the land from the Dutch and the force was successful.

Like many stories of American tradition the method used by the Dutch in taking Manhattan Island is subject to historical review. The popular story is that the Dutch cheated the Indians by taking Manhattan for $24 worth of trinkets. But there is another story. The Indians who made the deal were Carnarsie Indians from the lower part of Long Island, now known as Brooklyn—and they had no right to be on Manhattan, much less sell it.

In any case, the British took over the area and the Dutch continued to move upstream while the other nationalities jammed into the lower part of the small island off the American coast.

Lord Baltimore sailed from England, assured that his land grant was a wonderful place, and he found himself and his settlers in the inhospitable climate of Newfoundland. He headed south and took over what is now Maryland. William Penn accepted a grant in lieu of payment for a debt and brought his Quakers to Sylvania—the King in signing the charter added the "Penn," honoring the Quaker leader's father who was one of England's great fighting admirals.

From all of these and others, such as James Oglethorpe who founded Georgia and the Carolinas, came the establishment of the colonies on the eastern coast of North America.

The Spanish influence was still felt in the southern sections, the French were moving in through Canada, but the Anglo-Saxons pushed ahead with great zeal on the beachhead reaching from Maine to Virginia.

As the beachhead grew, the land-conscious people moved away from the coast. During the first days of the colonies the settlers were willing to trade with the Indians, obtaining whatever furs and produce the natives would give in exchange for nearly worthless beads and other gadgets.

The people who first clung to the shores of Plymouth, Boston, Salem and other small compounds soon took courage and moved inland. In the first decades of colonization, however, they moved slowly—first out to Dorchester, or perhaps to Jamaica Plain—or even out to Dedham, about 10 miles from the center of Boston.

The building techniques of the time differed from area to area. The famed log cabins of American history came from several sources. The Pilgrims devised a number of houses, the earliest with thatched roofs and those coming along a few years later with shingles. According to tradition, the Swedes and the Finns who first settled in Delaware began the idea of laying logs horizontally. From this has come various types of architecture in the United States. There are several 20th century versions of these old houses by 20th century designers—but often the original homes remain.

In New England one can find many homes built in the middle of the 17th century or the 18th century. Some are still in excellent condition and are the proud possessions of young families.

In that part of the nation the Fairbanks House in Dedham is the oldest wood-framed residence. Ten generations of the family of Jonathan Fairbanks, who came over from England in 1633, have lived in this house.

The first section of the house, often described as the "finest example of 17th century architecture in America" was built shortly after the arrival of the Fairbanks family in Dedham, then known as "Contentment." In 1648 the west wing was added and six years later another addition was put onto the house. An underground tunnel extends from the kitchen to a meadow down the road. It may have been used for many purposes; as a hiding place in case of Indian attack or as part of the "underground railroad" during the 19th century.

Kitchen, Fairbanks House built in 17th century, Dedham, Massachusetts.

The Indians in the vicinity were not particularly fierce and it is known that on occasion they came to sit around on the kitchen floor, smoke their pipes, waiting to be fed by the Fairbanks.

From the house have come many statesmen, clergymen, industrialists and inventors, along with frontier soldiers who fought to gain the West. One of the most noted members of the family was Charles Warren Fairbanks who was Vice President under Theodore Roosevelt.

Eventually the people seeking new homes moved along the rivers. The Dutch sought to colonize the Hudson River valley; those moving out from Boston found new havens along the Charles River, the Merrimack and the Mystic.

By the middle of the 17th century villages were being set up on the Connecticut River. The most famous is Deerfield which survived a tragic history and is today one of the shrines retained to remind Americans of the struggle our forefathers carried on to survive.

In 1675 Indians attacked the settlement and more than 50 soldiers and workmen, bringing supplies to Hadley, were slain at Bloody Brook. The village was abandoned for several years, but by 1682 settlers were returning and new homes were built.

The village was not destined to have peace for long. On February 29, 1704, a Major Hertel de Rouville led a force of 50 French and 200 Canadian Indians against the village slumbering on a winter night. Of the 291 inhabitants 48 were killed and 111 were taken prisoner. The captives were marched 300 miles over ice and snow to Quebec. Several years later about half the prisoners were returned, but others, some of whom were children when captured, chose to remain with the Indians.

Eunice Williams who was only seven years old when taken captive did not return to Deerfield until she was a middle-aged woman. Her stay was brief; she complained that she was not used to the luxury of beds and a roof over her head, and so she returned to the Abenaki tribe.

Sudden forays by marauding Indians were not uncommon and all homes were equipped with heavy wooden shutters which could be closed from the inside to protect the house from flying arrows.

As the villages moved farther and farther from the control of royal governors and other legal rulers of the colony, they found the need for a local type of government. From this need came the town meeting.

Some historians contend that the meeting in the captain's quarters aboard the *Mayflower* as she lay in the lee of Cape Cod in December 1620, was the first town meeting. It is a fact that a group of men got together and decided for themselves the rules that would govern them ashore. The honors, however, would seem to go to Dorchester where a call went out for a town meeting in 1634. The system of government was adopted in all the villages and towns of New England as the settlers moved out into the wilderness.

Traditionally the town meeting is held early in March. In colonial days, and indeed up until recently, the date was chosen with the realities of farm living in mind. Once the crops were harvested, the wood piled in the shed

(Continued on page 91)

Oak Alley, Vacherie, Louisiana.

U.S.S. Constitution, Boston Harbor.

Original costumes, Jamestown, Virginia.

Alamo at night, San Antonio, Texas.

Ancient Indian writings, Columbia River, Washington.

Civil War cannon, Cemetery Ridge, Pennsylvania.

White House, Washington Monument, Jefferson Memorial, Washington, D. C.

Independence Square, Philadelphia.

Statue of Liberty, New York Harbor.

and the cold winds began to sweep across the land, New Englanders stayed close to their firesides, going outdoors only to care for the livestock. But when the rigors of winter began to subside, when the snows melted and sent streams and rivers rushing in full flood toward the ocean, the New Englanders were ready to greet the season. The fields were still bitten with frost, making planting impossible, but the roads, although muddy, were passable.

The town meeting was more than a council of town fathers. It was a social affair as well. Once the constables had gone out with the town warrant warning one and all to attend "fail not at your peril," the families began preparations for the big day.

The women prepared their special dishes, the children looked forward to seeing friends, the men mulled over their orations, most of them had at least one article in the warrant that they were definitely for, or against.

Unlike other governing bodies the town meeting let every man have his say. Only the moderator could gavel him down. If you wanted a new bridge over the stream that led to your farm you stood up and told the rest of your neighbors the need for such construction, hoping to convince them. If you objected to an increase in the appropriation for an addition to the town hall you stood up and gave your reasons.

Down through the centuries the town meeting, like so many other institutions, however, has undergone a number of changes. But those who have moved into New England from other sections of the country are amused at the old-fashioned meeting, at the elections of "fence-viewer," "tree warden" and many of the other picturesque goings on. But with New Englanders it is still deadly serious.

The board of selectmen administer the town along with other elected officials throughout the year, but during the first week in March they have to answer to their fellow townsmen. Paved roads and automobiles have ended the winter isolation of the people, but the date is still kept.

The debates are just as vigorous as they ever were and the appropriations, like those at every other level of government, are scaled a good deal higher. If the debate is too slow the moderator may order the doors locked and inform the citizens that they will have to remain until the business is completed; or he may find the lack of a quorum and send the constables out into the streets to find enough citizens to satisfy the law.

Although it has survived many changes, the town meeting has undergone its biggest change in the decades since the end of World War II. The rush to the suburbs made many towns so large that it was impossible to accommodate all in any available auditorium. This led to the limited town meeting. Members are elected to represent a group of their neighbors.

In some instances the meeting can be carried on from week to week with the discussions wending their way endlessly through hours of long argument. In other cases the meeting can decide to appoint a committee to make a further study of a particular problem and then call a special town meeting for discussion of one problem alone, although in most instances several other odds and ends are also included.

Meetinghouse, Sturbridge Village, Massachusetts.

Paul Revere and Old North Church, Boston.

The Revolutionary War and Westward Expansion

The Paul Revere House in Boston's North Square may be the only 17th-century dwelling still standing in any large American city. The house was almost 100 years old when Revere purchased it in 1770. It has been restored and today is one of the major attractions on Boston's Freedom Trail. Hidden as it is among the maze of tenements in one of the oldest parts of the city even Bostonians are liable to get lost trying to locate it.

When one goes through the house one wonders where all of the numerous Revere children slept. The two-story structure with its overhang is hardly commodious by today's standards. But it was adequate for Revere who at the time was the city's leading silversmith and one of its leading patriots. Although most of his fame centers on the ride of the "18th of April in '75," immortalized by Longfellow, Revere was also active in many other mysterious goings-on in those days.

He was one of the inner circle in the Sons of Liberty who managed to keep things stirred up after passage of the Stamp Act in the 1760's. He drew a sketch of the Boston Massacre of March 5, 1770, and some historians believe he was on the scene, but there is no proof of this.

Revere's first known adventure as a courier for the Sons of Liberty came late in 1773 when he rode out of Boston to warn a number of surrounding towns that Boston was determined to stop the delivery of tea from the British ships in the harbor. On December 16, 1773, the word was given and 342 cases of tea were dumped overboard from three ships. The deed was hardly completed before Revere was on his way to New York and Philadelphia with the news.

When the port of Boston was closed in retaliation for the famed Tea Party, Revere was called on to ride to Portsmouth, New Hampshire, to warn local militia that British troops were coming to reinforce the harbor fort.

He got there first and the militia took over the fort, stripped it of gunpowder and other supplies.

Although Longfellow's poetic description of the famous "midnight ride" is less than historically accurate, it has served to stir the minds of generations. Revere had lanterns hung in the steeple of the Old North Church to warn the people of Charlestown of the coming of British troops; he then rode to Lexington to warn Samuel Adams and John Hancock, but he never did reach Concord. He was intercepted, along with William Dawes, after leaving Lexington and British soldiers took away his borrowed horse. One can only wonder what the history of this country might have been had Revere failed in his mission to warn Adams and Hancock.

Revere continued his work as a silversmith and goldsmith with a number of interruptions. He was commissioned at one time to make paper money for Massachusetts and is known to have tried his hand at making false teeth.

Revere, the skilled artisan, living in his tiny house on a market square; Hancock, the wealthy merchant, living in his splendid town house on Beacon Hill; Sam Adams, the fomenter of revolution, ekeing out a precarious existence; and in far off Virginia, George Washington, the gentleman plantation owner — all were bound together in a common purpose.

If Revere's house was hardly able to contain his ever expanding family, Washington's sumptuous Virginia mansion, Mount Vernon, was more than adequate for himself, his family and his servants.

During the long struggle for independence he often expressed the desire to return to the peaceful pursuits at Mount Vernon, but fate had decreed otherwise. After the war was won he was called on to work with the men framing the laws to govern this new land — and then he was called on to serve as the first President of the United States.

After the Declaration of Independence the struggle began in earnest

Washington's Home at Mt. Vernon, Virginia.

and it dragged on for five years. The first phase came to a close with the Battle of Saratoga, New York, on October 17, 1777. But it was preceded by the disastrous campaign of the British General John Burgoyne.

The military "geniuses" in London came up with a plan to cut the colonies in two by sending Burgoyne down from Montreal with an army which would join up with General Sir William Howe marching up the Hudson from New York City. The London military experts forgot one important point: There were no roads along the proposed route and Burgoyne soon bogged down. Howe, on the other hand, decided that instead of marching up to join with Burgoyne, he would create a diversion by attacking Philadelphia, capital of the foundling nation. That was his mistake; Washington had no intention of defending the city. The Continental Army was defeated at the Battle of the Brandywine. The Congress moved out of Philadelphia and the British moved in. Then the reports of Burgoyne's defeat at Saratoga brought the French into the fray on the side of the colonies.

That winter of 1777 was an ordeal for Washington, suffering in the intense cold at Valley Forge, begging for troops to remain until spring and pleading with the Congress for funds to pay the reluctant soldiers. It was the darkest hour of the Revolution, but out of it came an army hardened to privation and more determined than ever to fight on to victory. In 1779-1780, the stamina of the Continental Army was further molded by another trying winter, this one spent in Morristown, New Jersey. The Ford Mansion, which Washington used as his headquarters, still stands.

There was a slackening of the pace after Valley Forge, but hostilities started again in the South and came to a resounding climax at the Battle of Yorktown when Lord Cornwallis was defeated in October, 1781, and the war was virtually over with the American troops the victors. But the victors of what? The task of building a new nation lay before them. The major task was to keep the 13 colonies, fused in war, as one in peace. It was not an easy task.

Ford Mansion, Morristown, New Jersey.

The first attempt at building a nation was through the Articles of Confederation. The individual states wanted to keep as much power as possible. They sought to impose their own taxes and make their own money. It soon became apparent that such a system would only lead to disaster and lay the country open to a take-over by any foreign power.

On May 13, 1787, General George Washington arrived in Philadelphia to the thundering of artillery and the pealing of bells. He was greeted by the wealthy Robert Morris, known as "the Financier" and Superintendent of Finance under the Articles, who led Washington to one of the city's great mansions. Once his baggage was unloaded the General headed down Market Street to pay a call on Benjamin Franklin, one of the great symbols of the Revolution. Twelve days later the Constitutional Convention began in Independence Hall, where the Declaration of Independence had been adopted in 1776. This was a few days later than the opening session had been scheduled and James Madison of Virginia put these days to good use. He drafted a set of proposals, which substantially became the Virginia Plan that was presented by Governor Randolph to the Convention on May 29. Elaborated upon and refined, it was this Virginia Plan which became the Constitution of the United States.

Twelve states sent 55 delegates and they sat for four months. The document that came out of the long and vigorous discussions established a carefully worked out system of checks and balances, the basic elements of states' rights and Federal prerogatives. It established the nation that today is the oldest republic in the world. The first ten amendments — known as the Bill of Rights — which expressly protect the rights of the individual, were added a little later to put the finishing touches to the great document.

The Constitution has been the subject of discussion ever since it was adopted. As the country grew and new problems had to be faced it was amended from time to time. It remains, however, basically the same document and is now the law of the land in a nation of nearly 200 million, the same as it was for the 13 states hugging the Atlantic seaboard in the late 18th century.

Although there had been some westward movement before the Revolution it was confined mostly to speculators and hunters like Daniel Boone. Those who ventured beyond the mountains brought back stories of giant forests, vast buffalo herds and fertile land. Even before the Revolution, Boone and his companions were exploring the Kentucky area. They settled several towns, but constant harassment by Indians sent most of the settlers back to the comparative safety of the colonies nearer the ocean. Boone persisted and even moved to the area known as Upper Louisiana, now part of Missouri, where he built a home.

Others began moving west along various paths and trails. The first major breakthrough came with the building of the National Road or "Cumberland Road" in 1811. The opening of the road marked the beginning of the trek to the Northwest Territory. Less than ten years after the "highway" (although today it hardly seems worthy of the term) opened, it was reported that more than 15,000 people were moving over it annually from Philadelphia and Baltimore to the Ohio area.

Then New Yorkers conceived the idea of a canal connecting the Hudson River with the Great Lakes, opening up the entire middle of the country. Without much know-how and with tremendous engineering obstacles to overcome (such as moving over levels 600 feet above the sea) the Erie Canal was built and went into operation in 1825.

In the years preceding the opening of the 19th century the United States was involved in difficult struggles. Domestic problems of money, interpretation of the Constitution and trading among the states plagued the young nation. In the foreign field European nations were still reluctant to believe that a new and untried country had been formed across the ocean. They harassed American ships and in North Africa even enslaved American seamen — but not for long.

The world was startled by the American defiance of the Bey of Tunis, and England was later startled by American insistence on freedom of the seas.

The War of 1812 was caused by Great Britain's aggressive maritime policy in her war with Napoleon and by her alliance with the Indian tribes of the American Northwest. The first year of the American land campaign was a disaster, but Americans took heart from the capture of the 49-gun British frigate *Guerrière* by the *U.S.S. Constitution,* affectionately known as "Old Ironsides." The Lake Erie frontier was rewon in 1813, but the defeat of Napoleon in Europe freed a large number of British troops for a final offensive in America.

Chesapeake Bay had, in effect, become a British lake and the British veterans easily captured Washington, D. C., in August 1814. Baltimore was next on the British timetable. On September 12, a force of 4,000 troops landed at North Point and moved rapidly toward the city. By the next morning the British had moved within two miles of Baltimore and awaited the arrival of the fleet before storming the city. At dawn 16 enemy ships anchored in the river about two miles below Fort McHenry. During the hours that followed a barrage of 1,500 to 1,800 bombs and rockets was fired at the fort. On the 14th, a British landing party was driven off and, when the British admiral notified the army that hulks sunk by the Americans to block the entrance to North West Branch (an inlet leading directly to the city) prevented his giving naval support, the British withdrew. One month later the British left Chesapeake. General Andrew Jackson's victory at New Orleans in January 1815 came two weeks after the signing of a treaty ending the war.

The battle of Fort McHenry had been witnessed by Francis Scott Key, a lawyer. The emotions felt by Key that dawn as he saw the American flag still flying caused him to write a poem, "The Defense of Fort McHenry," that same day. Soon the poem was sung to the music of "To Anacreon in Heaven," an English song, and in 1931 Congress officially declared "The Star-Spangled Banner" our national anthem.

When the British captured Washington, D.C., in 1814 they burned the White House, home of American Presidents while in office. Designed by

Fort McHenry, *War of 1812 landmark, Maryland.*

Evergreen, *early 19th-century plantation, Louisiana.*

James Hoban, an Irish-born architect, it had been the first public building in the capital. The cornerstone was laid in 1792, and it was first occupied by President and Mrs. John Adams in November 1800. After the burning, only the sandstone walls and interior brickwork remained, but it was ready for occupancy by President James Monroe in 1817. Through the years the addition of porticos, balconies and modern conveniences have only enhanced this venerable building. The gentle simplicity and grace of its lines and the purity of its color, compared to the great palaces of the heads of state of other powerful nations, past and present, are impressive both to Americans and to the people of other lands.

The purchase by the United States of the vast province of Louisiana from France in 1803, the subsequent expedition by Meriwether Lewis and William Clark through the West and the defeat of the British set the stage for the great westward expansion beyond the Mississippi during the following decades. It also was the beginning of an increasingly violent antagonism between the self-dependent North and the slave-holding South, as both free farmers and planters with their slaves rushed into the West.

Cotton was "king" in the American South from 1815 to 1861 and slavery, the peculiar institution, as it was called by some, was the principal support of the king's throne. As people of the Western world began wearing cotton in place of wool and linen, the economy of the South prospered; its cotton crop doubled between 1820 and 1830. This and the ever greater subsequent growth was made possible by the expansion of the cotton growing area.

Cotton growing moved from South Carolina and Georgia across the "black belts" of soil in the Gulf states into the Mississippi and up to Memphis. By the 1850's cotton comprised more than half the value of all American exports. Three-quarters of the total world's supply of cotton, it was estimated, was furnished by the Gulf states, most of it shipped from New Orleans. This city also became the world's leading market for slaves.

The conditions of slavery and of the slaves differed widely; so did the attitude toward both. "The Negro cabins were small, dilapidated and dingy . . . and there were no windows," wrote Frederick Law Olmsted, a northern author. A southern lady, on the other hand, saw slaves villages "of small, whitewashed wooden houses . . . each house standing detached in its little garden." It was not, however, the living conditions but the "lot" of the slaves that was at issue. The very idea of slavery itself was abhorrent to men like George Washington, Thomas Jefferson and even General Robert E. Lee, simply because they believed in and fought for freedom for everybody from overlordship by anybody else. The stumbling block was economic and by that time very complex.

There can be no question, however, that life on the plantation was extremely comfortable for those who could benefit from this economic system. The plantations along the Mississippi River were particularly impressive. Within about 200 miles of New Orleans, in sight of each other on both sides of the river, were the magnificent plantation houses — tall, white and grandly pillared. The classic pattern was for the main house to face the Mississippi and between the house and the landing there was frequently an *allée* of fine trees, such as there still is at the plantation known as Oak Alley in Louisiana. There a tunnel of oaks 300 yards long was planted by a French pioneer in 1690 and they were fully grown by the time the house was built in 1832. On either side of the typical house were *garconnières* for guests. In the rear were gardens flanked by dovecotes. Beyond were the carriage houses, the long rows of slave quarters and the cotton gin or sugar mill. The largest plantations contained as many as 75 rooms and could accommodate 50 guests at a time. This ante-bellum South has well been called America's last great nonurban culture.

Part of the nation's westward expansion was the settlement of Texas, which began in 1821 when Moses Austin secured a charter from the government of New Spain for colonization by 300 American families. In 1824 Texas was made a state in the Mexican Republic and Texas was thrown open to colonization. A procession of revolutionary governments, however, resulted in the prohibition of colonization and the restriction of other rights. In 1833 a convention of Texans resolved to separate from Mexico. Relations between Texans and Mexicans worsened and armed clashes occurred. Dictator Santa Anna of Mexico raised an army of 6,000 and marched against the Texans in 1836. On February 23, 1836, Santa Anna and his army appeared at San Antonio. Lt. Colonel William Barret Travis in joint command, with James Bowie, of 145 men could have retreated, but instead moved into the stout-walled Alamo Mission. They answered a demand for surrender with cannon fire. A message from Travis read: "I have sustained a continual bombardment and cannonade for 24 hours and have not lost a man. . . . Our flag still proudly waves from the wall. I shall never surrender or retreat. VICTORY OR DEATH." His only reinforcements were 32 recruits who crept through Mexican lines on the eighth day of the battle. On the morning of March 6, the Mexicans stormed the Alamo on all sides. The first and second waves were stopped, but the Texan's guns were hot, they were almost out of ammunition and the men were dropping from exhaustion. The third assault breached the walls and the Texans, using knives and clubbing with their rifles, fought from room to room. The last fighting took place in the church where fell the legendary David Crockett and 12 volunteers who had followed him from Tennessee. The last of the defenders were dead. The Mexicans lost about 1,500.

As a consequence, the Texans under the redoubtable Sam Houston were galvanized into action and, with the cry, "Remember the Alamo," on their lips, they crushed the Mexicans at San Jacinto in April and established the Republic of Texas.

Throughout this time there were other kinds of expansion, and ships from the Eastern seaports started roaming the world. Today in Salem; Boston; Mystic, Connecticut; Newport, Rhode Island; New York; Philadelphia; and other cities there are historic reminders of the days when ships left to trade in Africa, India and China.

In some of the Eastern seaports, notably New Bedford and Nantucket, off the coast of Massachusetts, the wealth of the seven seas was also making

its mark. But here the men left to go in search of a specific source of wealth — whales. And the women who stayed behind watched for their return from a small fenced walkway on top of the home overlooking the ocean. Often the watch was long and lonely — a week, a month, a year — and the captain's wife could be seen each day pacing the small enclosure, often in vain. And so to this day the railed area atop a New England home is known as the "Widow's Walk."

In the middle of the 19th century a man named Colonel E. A. Drake drove a hole in the ground in western Pennsylvania and discovered a crude dark substance that made it unnecessary to travel half-way around the world for whale or other oil to light homes and factories. Where once man strove to find gold he now also sought oil. Its discovery changed the entire world and its refinement brought a new way of life. But it also brought depression to New Bedford and Nantucket. The latter was content to slumber along until vacationers found it to be a quaint place for a vacation. New Bedford, however, looked around and found the textile industry was booming. Thousands of immigrants from England came over to man the mills and the city once again became prosperous.

The Civil War and After

On March 4, 1861, Abraham Lincoln of Illinois was inaugurated President of the United States before a tense and uneasy throng. Several Southern states had threatened to secede if he became President. In his inauguration address he said: I have no purpose, directly or indirectly, to interfere with the institution of slavery where it exists." On the other hand, he said: "No state, upon its own mere motion, can lawfully get out of the Union. . . . Physically speaking, we cannot separate."

Probably no American has been written about as much as Abraham Lincoln. He stands astride the most crucial juncture of American history like a giant, a strong but gentle benefactor, part myth, part man. Unlike some folk heroes, however, Lincoln the man is almost as admirable and much more interesting than the myth, although of course more complicated.

On the surface Lincoln usually gave the appearance of a relatively simple man, but his personality was in many respects a puzzle and a paradox. He was ambitious and self-confident; his boyhood ambition had been to become President. But if Lincoln was not a modest man, he was a sincerely humble and magnanimous one, humble before what he called Divine Providence and the movements of history, magnanimous in his treatment of others, both the helpless and the powerful. He was also a compassionate man but he kept his compassion under control so that it did not conflict with his duty as a leader to see reality clearly, balanced, and as a whole. Two other important qualities of Lincoln were his perseverance and his integrity, both of which he displayed throughout his life.

When he left Springfield, Illinois, for his inauguration he said without exaggeration: "I now leave . . . with a task before me greater than that which rested upon Washington. Without the assistance of that Divine Being, who ever attended him, I cannot succeed. With that assistance I cannot fail."

Although his inaugural speech was peaceful in tone, he had decided several months before against any compromise of principle. Compromise, he knew, was no guarantee of peace. "The tug has to come, and better now than any time hereafter," he said.

Once he had determined not to surrender Fort Sumter, where the first shots of the Civil War were fired, he did not hesitate to prosecute the war, for he believed the war was a test to see if the American experiment of people governing themselves could successfully maintain itself while suppressing rebellion. He was convinced that the fate of world democracy hung on the fate of the Union. Such is the essence of his Gettysburg address.

At the beginning of the war, the South was much better prepared than the North and had a greater unity of purpose — independence. The North, however, had superiority in transportation, industry and population. Lincoln had to endure the inabilities of political generals such as Ben Butler because they controlled sizable segments of public opinion, but this was not as much of a hindrance as was the lack of a viable central government to the Confederacy. Once the Federal Government in Washington was organized — particularly the War Department under the irascible but efficient Edwin M. Stanton — the Union superiority began to be felt.

What was needed finally was a general who could command the Union armies to decisive victories. Lincoln patiently sifted through a series of generals, relieving each in turn. During this period Lincoln visited the Army of the Potomac repeatedly to confer with its commanders, but most of Lincoln's involvement in military matters proved unsuccessful, usually due to political pressures or unsatisfactory personnel. This involvement ceased when Lincoln found, in late 1862, the general-in-chief whom he had been seeking: Ulysses S. Grant, a fellow-Midwesterner, with a reputation for drinking and getting things done.

A graduate of West Point, Grant fought bravely in the Mexican War, but after the war he tired of dreary post duty and resigned from the army. Unsuccessful in various occupations, at the outbreak of the Civil War he was a clerk in his brother's leather shop in Galena, Illinois. He applied to Washington for duty but received no reply; however, he was appointed colonel of the 21st Illinois Volunteers. Later promoted to brigadier general, his capture of Fort Henry and Fort Donelson in 1862 and his refusal to accept any terms other than unconditional surrender, brought a promotion from Lincoln to major general. His lack of leadership at Shiloh caused much criticism, but he redeemed himself at the crucial battle of Vicksburg, Mississippi, the capture of which gave the Union control of the Mississippi River. He was then awarded the command of all Union armies.

The turning point in the war is generally thought to have been Gettysburg. With the possible exception of D-Day 1944, probably no American battle has seared itself into the American national memory as has the struggle at Gettysburg, Pennsylvania. It was brought about by Confederate commander Robert E. Lee's decision — made partly in hope of winning foreign recognition, partly to encourage dissension and appeasement in the

West Point cadets on parade, New York.

North — to carry the war to the enemy. The battle was decided on the third day, July 3, 1863, when three gray lines of Confederates charged Cemetery Ridge. They were shattered with artillery and musket fire. Less than half a company reached the crest of Cemetery Ridge, where most were killed or captured, while a few turned and escaped. Lee retired from the area the next day.

On November 19 the cemetery at Gettysburg was dedicated and the brief address Lincoln delivered there can be said to have begun the rebirth of the nation: ". . . From these honored dead we take increased devotion to that cause for which they gave the last full measure of devotion . . . we here highly resolve that these dead shall not have died in vain; that this nation, under God, shall have a new birth of freedom; and that government of the people, by the people, for the people shall not perish from the earth."

The war dragged on for several more months, but the outcome was inevitable. On April 9, 1865, General Lee surrendered to General Grant in the front parlor of McClean House at Appomattox Courthouse, Virginia. Lee's soldiers were paroled to return home, officers were permitted to retain sidearms and all soldiers allowed to retain private horses and mules.

Good Friday, April 14, 1865, was a brilliant spring day. Lincoln rose early as usual and was in his office by about seven. During the morning he met with General Grant and the cabinet. Grant described his final drive of the war and gave details of General Lee's surrender five days before. Lincoln spoke kindly of Lee and other Confederate officers and said he hoped there would be no persecutions, "no bloody work," because enough blood had been shed.

After lunch Lincoln signed a pardon for a deserter saying, "the boy can do us more good above ground than under ground," and he revoked the death sentence of a Confederate spy. By four in the afternoon Lincoln escaped from his office for a quiet drive with Mrs. Lincoln. He spoke of their life ahead: "We must both be more cheerful in the future. Between the war and the loss of our darling Willie (referring to their son who had died three years before) , we have both been very miserable."

Because of seeing visitors that evening the Lincolns finished dinner late. Then with friends they went to the theatre to see Laura Keene in *Our American Cousin*. They arrived at Ford's Theatre 15 minutes later, and the performance stopped as the Lincoln party entered its box. Lincoln acknowledged the cheers as he dropped into the haircloth rocking chair at the rear of the box. A guard assigned to protect the President sought a seat where he could watch the play.

In the third act Lincoln was enjoying the play immensely as Mrs. Lincoln reached out and took the hand of her husband. Then the audience below heard a muffled shot and a scream from the box; a man hurtled to the stage shouting something that sounded like "Sic semper tyrannis" ("Thus always to tyrants"), the motto of Virginia, and then hurried off stage dragging his left leg. The man was actor John Wilkes Booth.

Lincoln was carried across the street from the theatre to the modest home of William Peterson, a tailor. Dawn brought a cold rain, and a silent crowd stood outside the home as rumors spread throughout Washington of plots against the lives of General Grant and Vice President Andrew Johnson. After holding on to life stubbornly for a few hours Lincoln died at 7:22 A.M.

A nation that had been born in violence was reborn in violence. But the bloody struggle, for all its wantonness and waste, somehow had seemed to prepare the nation for the beginnings of greatness. The catastrophe of brother killing brother seemed to mature the national conscience. At any rate, from that time, America walked with a more confident stride and spoke with a surer voice. There were many struggles ahead, more progress to be made, more injustices to be painfully corrected. But the men and boys who had died had shown what sacrifice could achieve, and the leader who had been given up to death was not the last of his kind either.

The turmoils of Reconstruction and the final step of westward expansion to the frontiers of the "Wild West" followed the war. Despite the troubles, however, the tide of humanity still moved toward these shores. Somehow the human mind found the meaning of this wild new adventure that lay across the Atlantic. Somehow, even the quarreling elements already here sensed it.

It was best brought to both by a verse, written by an American Jewish poetess, Emma Lazarus, which is now inscribed on the base of the Statue of Liberty, a gift from the French people, which was dedicated at Bedloe's Island in New York Harbor on October 28, 1886:

> "Give me your tired, your poor,
> Your huddled masses yearning to breathe free,
> The wretched refuse of your teeming shore.
> Send these, the homeless, tempest-tost, to me,
> I lift my lamp beside the golden door!"

From that day to this the gallant lady has been a symbol of the freedom and liberty of this land. Never has an immigrant arrived nor an American come back from overseas, who has not felt a sense of uplift and pride as his ship pulled into view of this towering symbol.

As the population grew, the industrial power of the country grew. The strange inventions of Bell and Ford and Edison and the Wright Brothers developed into huge industries employing millions of people. The factories required hundreds of ancillary units to keep them going. All working together brought out of the late 19th century a nation unlike any ever seen on the face of the earth.

United Nations, New York.

Iwo Jima-Marine monument,
Washington, D. C.

The times were not without their troubles. There was the Spanish-American War during which the nation moved out of its shell to become a part of the world scene and to accept new responsibilities. The indefatigable Theodore Roosevelt, who fought in that war, later became President and was in many ways the ideal leader for the United States during its first years as a world power. He was one of the four great Presidents whose likenesses were carved out of the granite of South Dakota's Black Hills in the later 1920's and 30's to form the inspiring Mount Rushmore National Memorial. Washington, Jefferson and Lincoln are the others depicted there.

World War I found American troops fighting in France. The valor of the Marines on the Argonne and in Belleau Wood is part of our tradition. The valor of American fliers such as those in the famed 94th "Hat-in-the-Ring" Squadron of Captain Eddie Rickenbacker, the men who flew with the Lafayette Escadrille, and the first bombardiers will live on in memory.

They fought to make the "world safe for democracy"; they were buried with honor in Arlington National Cemetery on the bank of the Potomac. But their fight, in part, was in vain. President Woodrow Wilson's attempt to persuade the United States to join the League of Nations was unsuccessful (although his courageous attempt was later to serve as the touchstone for American backing of the United Nations in 1945). Europe was left in a shambles. In the colossus that is Russia, communism took over; in defeated Germany the bewildered people turned to a madman named Adolph Hitler.

The impact was felt in the United States, where the Great Depression

Soldier's burial, Arlington National Cemetery, Virginia.

started in 1929 and lasted through the first half of the next decade. While experimenting, in the American tradition, with possible new solutions to social and economic problems, the United States adhered faithfully to the original principles of the Constitution of the Founding Fathers; and it weathered the storm.

Attacked by the Japanese at Pearl Harbor on December 7, 1941, a "day of infamy," as President Franklin D. Roosevelt called it, the nation again turned to the task. It was a challenge reluctantly accepted, since most Americans prefer to enjoy the affluence of life, rather than to dissipate its wonders through war.

Some other nations mistook this attitude for one of weakness — an opinion that was soon discarded as the great might of the nation arose to face the aggressors. It was then that the militant dictators of Japan, Germany and Italy found that the Americans and their allies would fight magnificently for freedom when aroused to the necessity for doing so.

The citizen-soldiers who starved on Corregidor, fought in the barren deserts of Africa, raised the flag triumphantly over Iwo Jima and waded ashore under blistering fire on the beaches of Normandy, did what they did so successfully, mostly because of what had been done by other Americans before them. They were fighting not to win a war, but to preserve freedom, freedom of many kinds, and to establish peace, the only environment in which freedom can flourish. It is a purpose that most Americans — whether in a uniform or not, whether Peace Corpsmen or Marine Corpsmen — cherish as the heart of their heritage.

Religious procession in the Washington Cathedral, Washington, D. C.

America is Worship and Knowledge

III

A Nation of Churchgoers

We wish that this column, rising towards heaven among the pointed spires of so many temples dedicated to God, may contribute also to produce in all minds a pious feeling of dependence and gratitude. — Daniel Webster

No matter what the nation's perhaps over-abundant materialistic distractions may be, there are still about 123 million Americans attending almost 322,000 local churches or congregations throughout this land.

America, very simply, is still a nation of churchgoers. In this country one just cannot escape the appeal and traditions of the houses of God. They are constantly before our eyes—in teeming cities, in quiet villages, at the confluence of deserts and mountains, and still clanging out their bells as the fishing boats sail home to ports like Gloucester, Massachusetts, and San Francisco, California.

There are 78 religious groups with 50,000 or more members of American churches, and these constitute 98 per cent of the total church membership in our nation. The remaining religionists constitute 172 relatively small groups. Some, like the Church of Christ, Scientist, do not report their membership because of regulated policy.

Of the total American church membership, 55 per cent is classified as Protestant, 37 per cent Roman Catholic, 4.5 per cent Jewish and 3.5 per cent of all other bodies including Buddhists and Eastern Orthodox, Muslims and other creeds.

The Roman Catholic Church, with its huge metropolitan city concentrations of members, is the largest religious group in the U. S. A., with over 45 million communicants. The various Baptist bodies across our land are the second largest "persuasion," with over 23 million members and their own geographical blocks topped by the 10.5 million co-religionists of the Southern Baptist Convention.

Several nations of the Western world have acquired at some time in their history a sense of mission. The United States was born with it. The twin streams of 18th century enlightenment, exemplified by Jefferson's concept of this nation as the world's model for democracy, and the millenarian impulse of New England Puritanism fed and nurtured that sense.

The millenarian impulse was first expressed by John Winthrop about 1630 when he spoke of his Massachusetts colony as "a city set upon a hill," a colony whose mission was to establish a pattern for all Christendom. In the 1740's, during the Great Awakening, Jonathan Edwards carried the expressions of Winthrop one step further with the statement that the millennium would "probably . . . begin in America."

Because European settlers brought their religious traditions with them there was, from the early 17th century, a diversity of religious bodies in this nation. Most of them — the Dutch Reformed in New Netherland, the Swedish Lutherans in Delaware and the Church of England in Virginia and other southern colonies — tried to curb dissent within their particular colony but were more or less unsuccessful for a variety of reasons, including the lack of sufficient clergymen to cover wide, sparsely settled areas. The Quakers in Pennsylvania made full provision for religious tolerance. In Maryland, where settlement had begun in 1634 as a refuge for Catholics, toleration was extended to all Christians; and Protestants outnumbered Catholics from the start. Small groups of English Baptists, who were devoted by principle to religious liberty, began arriving in New England in the late 1630's. In the mid-17th century small communities of Jews arose in Manhattan, Newport, Philadelphia and some southern cities. Thus diversity within each colony increased. Only the Puritans were able to establish a religious oligarchy that lasted for decades.

The eventual pattern of religion in America had been indicated in 1635 when, on October 9, clergyman Roger Williams, was found guilty of propagating dangerous opinions, namely that the Puritan oligarchy was oppressive and its civil government had no right to enforce religious injunctions. Magistrates were sent to arrest him but he was warned in advance and escaped and made his way to friendly Indians. After suffering privations he gathered enough followers to found Providence, the earliest Rhode Island settlement.

Religious liberty, in the opinion of many, is one of the greatest contributions that America has made both in the realm of politics and religion.

At the time the colonies were begun every country in Europe had a state church. Constitutional religious freedom and actual separation of church and state in America were the result of two factors working in a new country: the convictions of non-conformist groups and the conclusions—based on a study of history, political philosophy and the practical needs of a situation involving many divergent sects—reached by certain broad-minded statesmen, particularly James Madison, Thomas Jefferson and others in Virginia. The Constitutional Convention of 1787 to a large degree simply recognized a principle already in practical operation.

So the Puritan concept, a religious state, died in America. But the Puritan sense of mission did not die. As the West opened up in the early 19th century, Protestant church leaders launched the Second Great Awakening: Revivalism, a new phase of the errand in the wilderness. The camp meeting, the circuit rider, the itinerant preacher brought the Word of God to the brutish frontier. Partly as a result, a great slash of the nation, across the South and lower Midwest, is still known today as the Bible Belt. The suffering of the Mormons on their long trek from New York to Utah, where they arrived in 1847, has for many come to symbolize the firmness

Chamber, Touro Synagogue, Newport, Rhode Island.

Traditional New England church, rural Vermont.

109

St. Patrick's Cathedral and Atlas statue, New York City.

of the American religious sense of mission. And this sense was carried past the mid-19th century into the bloodiest of American wars as the Union army marched off to the stirring strains of Julia Ward Howe's "The Battle Hymn of the Republic."

Complete religious liberty did not, however, bring with it the elimination of religious prejudice. The conflicts between Protestant and Catholic have been especially bitter and the nation reached a notable milestone in its maturity when John F. Kennedy, a Catholic, was elected President in 1960.

Perhaps today the greatest visible sign of America's reverence for her religious past, present and future are the houses of worship, ancient and modern, across the land, "the pointed spires of so many temples. . . ." as Daniel Webster once phrased it.

To many Americans the phrase "the American church" immediately conjures up the scene of a little white New England church and there is probably no style of American architecture that has been so well preserved for so long. The Puritan meetinghouse was built in the center of the village and served not only for assembly on the Sabbath but also for town meetings and as a gathering place of the inhabitants at all times of peril or emergency. None of these is more famous than Boston's Old North Church where at ten o'clock on the night of April 18, 1775, Paul Revere, silversmith and engraver, had the sexton hang two lanterns in the tower to warn the Charlestown patriots that British troops were coming that way. There are, however, scores of others throughout New England, such as the handsome First Congregational Church, Old Lyme, Connecticut, which was built in 1817.

Among those who heard with gladness the news that Roger Williams had established a colony that practiced religious liberty were the Sephardic Jews of Spain and Portugal. They came to Newport in Williams' colony, perhaps as early as 1658, and were accepted. Their first community project was to build a cemetery plot in 1677. With the financial help of Jewish congregations in New York, Jamaica, Surinam and London, a synagogue was built and dedicated in 1763. It was designed by Peter Harrison, the most renowned American architect of his time, with the simplicity and restraint in keeping with the tradition of the Sephardim. Newport declined and the synagogue closed its doors before 1800. However, the descendants of the Rev. Isaac Touro, who had officiated at the synagogue's dedication, initiated a fund in the 1820's that restored the edifice, now called Touro Synagogue, and enabled it to be permanently reopened in 1883.

New York City, the center of so much that is American, is a repository of fine churches of virtually all denominations, from all periods and in all styles. The busy and sprawling, yet majestic Episcopal cathedral, St. John the Divine, is famous for its Boys' Choir School and an open air pulpit. It was designed in the Romanesque style, in 1892, by architects G. L. Heins and C. Grant La Farge, but oddly enough, the plans were changed in 1911 when Ralph Adams Cram entered the design picture, adopting the Gothic style. The entire length of the finished nave was finally opened in 1941, but even today the church is not yet completed. This beautiful

*Cathedral of St. John
the Divine, New York.*

repository of uninterrupted American worship of God, the favored place of spiritual sustenance for thousands of New Yorkers and throngs of visitors from all parts of the nation and the world, is as characteristic of Manhattan as the automat and is the ecumenical "twin" of the storied old Roman Catholic St. Patrick's Cathedral at 50th Street and Fifth Avenue.

Who can mention old St. Pat's, whose cornerstone was laid in 1858, without evoking mellow memories of decades of Irish political merriment in the St. Patrick's Day parade which annually troops by the cathedral? And certain names always come to mind in connection with this vast, marble, cruciform-shaped, Gothic structure. There is its world-renowned pastor, of course, Francis Cardinal Spellman, Roman Catholic Archbishop of New York, and globe-traveling chaplain of the armed forces. And names like the late New York Governor Al Smith and fabled Mayor Jimmy Walker, come to mind. For they, too, paraded along Fifth Avenue, past the wide cathedral porch on St. Patrick's Day.

And who can forget the vast outpouring of reverence and acclaim which arose mightily from the throngs which greeted Pope Paul VI in October of 1965 when he visited St. Patrick's and the United Nations. At St. Patrick's he strolled through its patios with Cardinal Spellman waving cordially at the office workers who thrilled to look down upon the Pontiff from their skyscraper towers of business; Giovanni Montini, 262nd Pope of Roman Catholicism, spoke from St. Patrick's high altar and sat in the rectory chair reserved for "popes alone." He won the hearts of all New York and the good will of the nation that day, and, sojourning at warm, well-loved St. Patrick's, he could not have gone to the United Nations from a more auspicious place.

At St. Patrick's he saw, as thousands have seen, year after year, the Lady Chapel behind the high altar, the 11 other side chapels, the great stained glass windows and, above him, the joyous chimes of 19 bells.

The cathedrals of our nation's capital are now more familiar to us because they have been the worshiping places of recent Presidents; we are familiar, because of massive TV coverage, with St. Mark's Catholic Cathedral where the late President Kennedy's Funeral Mass was celebrated and where he had once attended services. More recently we have been aware of the regular attendance of President and Mrs. Lyndon B. Johnson at Sunday services in the spacious National Episcopal Cathedral.

Yet it took the August 1966, marriage of President and Mrs. Johnson's daughter Luci to Patrick Nugent in the National Shrine of the Immaculate Conception to familiarize most Americans with the fact that this magnificent edifice is probably the largest church in the United States and has been called "the seventh largest" in the world.

The National Shrine project was begun in 1914, with the foundation stone being set in 1920. The crypt was completed six years later, and the upper church and superstructure dedicated in 1959. The dimensions are astounding: external length, 459 feet; external width, 250 feet; interior height, under the dome, 159 feet; seating capacity, 3,000; total capacity, 6,000. There are 50 altars in side chapels among which the Shrine of Our

Lady of Guadalupe is notable. This altar was donated by Richard Cardinal Cushing of Boston, out of his devotion to the missions and people of Latin America.

In the Midwest, Frank Lloyd Wright, whom many recognize as the greatest architect America has produced, designed a stunning church for the Greek Orthodox of Wisconsin, the state where he was born and came to maturity. In Wauwatosa, a suburb of Milwaukee, the circular Church of the Annunciation dominates a broad open space from atop a low sloping hill. Its bright blue roof, rounded in conformity with the hill, is iridescent in the sunlight, and the whole edifice speaks boldly of the intimate relationship possible between God and genius.

Easter service, Red Rocks Amphitheater, Colorado.

The Red Rocks Natural Amphitheater is located amid the splendors of the Rocky Mountain foothills, about 14 miles from Denver. The amphitheater has been carved into the side of rock formations that are rust-red in color and which stand out vividly among surroundings of green foliage, a background of gray, nearby mountain faces and the continually changing cloud formations that sail over the mountains from the west. The annual Red Rocks Easter service, which is interdenominational, is magnificent. The crowd gathers before sunrise for the service. As the first rays of light appear on the eastern horizon the service begins. Morning cloud formations often increase the dramatic quality of the sunrise, the cloud layers forming intermediate filters for the sunrise colors — gold at the horizon, then the pastel yellow which merges into the clear blue of a sky unveiled by a haze common to lower elevations.

Not many miles away is the Air Force Academy Chapel at Colorado

Springs. When it was built in 1962 it was quite controversial but its soaring testament is now an accepted masterpiece of modern American architecture.

Westward to the Great Salt Lake and the colorful religious center of Salt Lake City, where the "Latter Day Saints," as the Mormons are more formally known, built their great mother church, or Tabernacle. Its sonorous organ and hundred-throated golden choir are now familiar to the nation as one of the mighty voices of immutable Christianity in our land.

Southwesterly, we inevitably come upon the powerful religious residuals of the Spanish-Franciscan impact seen in Francisco Coronado's fabled yet futile search for "The Seven Cities of Cibola" and their legendary wealth in the early 16th century. He, like another Spanish conquistador, Hernando De Soto, who probed the Southwest and the mouth of the Mississippi, aided all unwittingly in the establishment of Spanish missions, helping all of us to become a nation of churchgoers.

San Xavier del Bac Mission, nine miles south of Tucson, is a magnificent Spanish Renaissance-style church, the sole intact survivor of the Arizona mission chain. Built by Franciscans between 1783 and 1803, its lovely baroque interior contains interesting native art work and religious objects.

Perhaps the most memorable of the Franciscans, in terms of his impact on American religious history, was Father Junipero Serra who, in the middle of the 18th century, established 21 missions along the mission trail immortalized as *El Camino Real*. His religious and educational impact on San Diego and Monterey in the Golden State endures into our own day.

Not all churches are great edifices, and the test of American religious faith is that the same humbling-before-God exists in the austere Quaker meeting house in the hills of Pennsylvania, the white clapboard Protestant church among the cornfields of Iowa or on the plains of South Dakota, the mammoth arena where evangelist Billy Graham holds meetings and the humble Baptist Negro "shack" in the Deep South.

In the words of St. Paul: "Extinguish not the spirit" the American churches seem to tell all Americans eternally. These residuals of our eternal belief came from Europe, Asia and Africa. In such a richly endowed people it would seem impossible for our solemn and multifarious houses of God to be less than pre-eminent as our prevailing point of contact with a wise, merciful and just God.

Education and the American Dream

In order to build a new country in the wilderness and to perpetuate the religious beliefs that brought so many of the first European settlers to these shores, Americans early became devoted to education. Today's massive elementary and secondary state and parochial school systems and world renowned universities such as Harvard, Columbia, Chicago, Stanford and the multiversities of the Midwest and California are the result of this constantly renewed devotion.

One-room schoolhouse, Leadville, Colorado.

Head Start students, Washington, D. C.

St. Martin's Academy, Rapid City, South Dakota.

Seventeenth-century England, Holland and Scotland (with its Calvinistic emphasis on universal education) all contributed important ideas to American education. But it was to develop along its own unique and highly original path.

In the earliest colonial period those children whose parents could not afford to pay were enabled, through apprenticeship laws passed by colonial legislatures, to obtain vocational training and the fundamentals of reading and religion. In 1647 the Massachusetts legislature passed the "Old Deluder Satan Act" which required each township of 50 families to engage a teacher to instruct children in reading and writing and each township of 100 families to establish a "grammar schoole" to fit youth for "ye university" under penalty of fine. Many historians consider this law, the expressed purpose of which was to frustrate the designs of "ye ould deluder Satan," to be the foundation for the American public school system. Education initiated in the peripheral regions of the colonial Northeast—the Southeast, the West and Southwest—was in accord with the precepts of the Catholic church.

The first colleges and universities founded in the Americas were religiously motivated and oriented. In 1538 Spanish missionaries founded on the Caribbean island of Hispaniola this hemisphere's earliest known university, the University of Santo Domingo; and Puritan ministers in 1636 established Newtowne College—later to be Harvard College—in that part of Cambridge, Massachusetts, earlier known as "Newtowne." Both groups formed their curricula and selected their staffs and students as components of a seminary or college of theology.

Harvard today has become a famed international university distinguished for liberal and emancipated views on religion and everything else; yet that institution still has a highly professional theological school. This pattern is evident across the continental United States where numerous colleges and universities owing their origins to theological motives have now expanded into widely secular areas. Many, however, still retain college units or study programs which orient future ministers and priests for the more formal disciplines of sacred studies.

Secondary education in New England began with the establishment of the Boston Latin School in 1635. Graduates of this and similar schools, which emphasized the teaching of Latin and Greek, were qualified for admission to Harvard College. Pennsylvania led the other Middle Colonies in the establishment of secondary education with the founding, in 1689, of the Friends' Public School of Philadelphia (now called William Penn Charter School).

Under Anglican auspices, King's College (now Columbia University), was established in 1754. The College of William and Mary, which did not grant degrees until 1700, was the only college in the South during the colonial period.

After the Revolution, proposals for a national school system based on democratic principles were made by Noah Webster and others, but went unheeded. It was Webster's *The American Spelling Book* that, in the

1840's, replaced, as the country's basic school textbook, the *New England Primer,* first published in 1690. Webster's *An American Dictionary of the English Language,* published in 1828, became a basis for American English.

The first state-chartered universities were in Georgia, North Carolina and Vermont, but only North Carolina granted degrees before the end of the 18th century. Government began its long and vital role in American education with the Northwest Ordinance of 1787 which provided that the 640-acre area designated Section 16 in every township in the Western territory be used for the purpose of public education.

New England, however, was the only region that could claim anything like a public school system in the years immediately following the Revolution. Only eight of the first 16 states inserted educational provisions into their constitutions. At this time the Latin grammar school gave way to the broader curriculum of the English grammar school and the academy, and finally the high school.

As the nation grew and became industrialized, labor groups and others began to demand a public school system. Education was becoming an imperative of the American dream of success and the good life. Through the efforts of Horace Mann and others, in 1837 Massachusetts set up a state board of education which introduced many reforms such as supervision and in-service training of teachers. In 1852 Massachusetts was the national leader in enacting legislation to make school attendance compulsory. Another important elementary school innovation was the kindergarten; the first English-speaking one was opened in Boston in 1860.

The Morrill Act of 1862 made land grants available to the states for the establishment of colleges where the "agriculture and the mechanic arts" would be taught along with military science and "other scientific and classical studies." This brought about the expansion of the state universities in the Midwest and Far West that play such a large role in American education today.

In the 19th century, parochial school systems were developed by the Lutherans, Episcopalians, Jews and Catholics. In 1884 the Catholic Bishops' Third Plenary Council decreed that all Catholic parents must send their children to parochial schools to be erected in all parishes. Catholic parochial schools now enroll about one-sixth of the country's elementary students.

With the 20th century came the startling educational ideas of John Dewey and the controversies of progressive education. The general feeling of most Americans that their educational system was the finest in the world was shaken, however, in 1957 with the Soviet Union's launching of its Sputnik satellite. The nation's response to what it felt was a direct challenge to the American system was as bold and even more substantial than its reactions to other educational crises throughout its history. Science was given a larger share of the secondary school curriculum, standards in all fields and at all levels were strengthened and the Federal Government, which had significantly increased its participation in education with the G.I. Bill of 1943-1944, became even more fully involved.

Hoover Tower, Stanford University, California.

Duke University campus, Durham, North Carolina.

Scientific education began to flourish in America with the founding in 1861 of the Massachusetts Institute of Technology. Today the nation's world leadership in most areas of science, including space, is led by that great institution and others, such as the Carnegie Institute of Technology in Pittsburgh, the Illinois Institute of Technology in Chicago, Rice University in Texas, and the California Institute of Technology in Pasadena, California.

America's advancement of the quality of its education during the past decade is all the more remarkable because it was done at the same time that a substantial increase in its overall productive capacity became necessary. In 1940 there were 30 million Americans of school age (five to 17 years old) ; by 1960 there were 43 million. This has meant record high expenditures for new schools and improved facilities. In addition, the Supreme Court's 1954 decision that segregation of the races in public schools was unconstitutional brought further turmoil. Better education for the Negro became an integral part of the effort to improve the education of all Americans.

One result of this improvement is that the one-room rural school house, hallowed by tradition and the greatness of some of its former students, has almost disappeared from the scene. In its place is the large, well-equipped consolidated school, serving the needs of a relatively wide area and providing an education the equal of that received in most cities and suburbs.

Another great contributor to American education through the decades, the small liberal arts college, is searching for ways to insure its continuing importance. In Ohio, Oberlin, even today one of the nation's outstanding schools, began coeducation in this country in 1833. Lawrence, at Appleton, Wisconsin, which just recently became a university, has furnished presidents for Harvard, Duke, Brown and several others. Most of these liberal arts colleges, often originally established for religious purposes, did not expand to the massive proportions of Harvard, Yale, Princeton and Stanford, for example. But for generations these smaller colleges maintained a general education concept, based on a synthesis of man's intellectual attainments, and produced more than their share of outstanding scholars and were significantly prominent in developing the competence of the professions of teaching, law and medicine, as well as maintaining healthy contributions to social and cultural standards throughout a cross-section of the nation. Williams College in Massachusetts and Haverford in Pennsylvania have been famous for generations for the excellence of their scholarship. More recently, Reed in Oregon and Pomona in California have attained the same position.

The great increase, however, in giant endowments, massive Federal and private foundation grants and research support has partially shifted the emphasis from the small college.

Typical of the myriad small liberal arts colleges is Miami University of Ohio, founded in 1809. Miami now has an impressive enrollment of almost 9,000 students but is only modestly endowed to the amount of $1,676,000. Dr. John D. Millett, former president of this university, and now chancellor of the Ohio Board of Regents, recently concluded that "preservation of the liberal arts college is tremendously important because its small enrollment, low student-faculty ratio and emphasis on teaching set standards for all undergraduate education." He believes, however, that the liberal arts college will continue to prosper if it can find answers to its problems of financing, staffing and curriculum. In order to accomplish this Dr. Millett is calling on Ohio, as other small colleges are doing similarly in other states, for a share of state tax funds—for grants-in-aid and for tuition grants ranging from $100 to $500 each to students at private colleges.

One of the most significant years in the history of American education was 1965. After 20 years of deadlock over general Federal aid to education, mainly because of the problem of aid to church-related schools, Congress was able to pass the pioneering Elementary and Secondary School Improvement Act and the Higher Education Act. The former provides for a total of $1.3 billion with $1.06 billion available to public schools in areas with

Schoolgirl, Illinois.

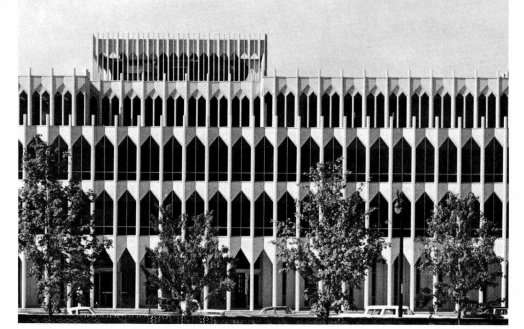

Education building, Wayne State University, Michigan.

College crowd, Wisconsin.

children from families whose incomes were $2,000 a year or less. The estimate at enactment time was that aid would be given to about five million children in virtually all school districts. The 1965 act also authorized some assistance to nonpublic, including parochial school, pupils.

The higher education measure provided $2.3 billion for 140,000 three-year Federal scholarships, called educational opportunity grants, for exceptionally needy and promising students. A two-year program for a national teacher corps was also authorized, under which 6,000 teachers would be recruited to serve in poverty areas.

So that the Negro might have a better opportunity to make use of education, as other ethnic groups have in the past, to obtain his fair share in the American dream, both Federal laws included fairly stringent criteria to prevent aid from going to segregated schools. In addition, Project Head Start began in 1965, offering more than 500,000 children in areas of poverty special preparation during the summer months just prior to their first year of elementary school.

In America today there are a total of 54.2 million students currently in school enrollment: 35.9 million of these are in kindergarten through grade 8; 12.9 million are in high school, grades 9 through 12; and 5.4 million are in higher education, all to benefit, whole or partially, by revolutionary, progressive, intellectual and financial aid, on the part of both the academic and legislative communities.

A few of these millions attend such famous secondary-level institutions as Boston Latin School, Bronx High School of Science, New Trier High School in Wilmette, Illinois, and Lowell High School in San Francisco or one of the outstanding private preparatory schools such as Choate in Connecticut and Culver Military Academy in Indiana. Most, however, go to one of the other thousands of high schools in the nation.

At the higher levels of education some students are fortunate enough to receive their education at one of the many truly beautiful campuses in the United States: Dartmouth in New Hamsphire, Princeton in New Jersey and Duke in North Carolina have almost perfect neat, wooded, ivy-accented appearances. Cornell's setting on the hills above Cayuga's waters in New York is legendary. Little Hanover College in Indiana, placidly placed high on the bluffs overlooking the Ohio River, is thought by many who have seen it to have the most beautiful campus in America. The University of Wisconsin on the tree-lined shores of Lake Mendota, dotted with sailboats most of the summer, wears the scenic crown of the Big Ten. And few universities can rival the spectacular backdrop the Rockies afford the University of Colorado. Many other students of course receive their degrees from great metropolitan universities such as the City University of New York, the University of Pittsburgh, Wayne State in Detroit and the University of California in Berkeley. But all of this means little beside what is being *taught* and learned in all of these schools.

Americans have long recognized that the claims of democracy to provide equal opportunity for all mean little without accessibility to education. Founding Fathers such as George Washington and Thomas Jefferson—who said, "Enlighten the people generally, and tyranny and oppressions of body and mind will vanish like evil spirits at the dawn of day"—were intensely aware of this fact. At the same time, there has seldom been any delusion that mass education necessarily meant quality education. The fact that both have been achieved is a tribute to the American pursuit of both quality and excellence. This quest for superior education was perhaps first expressed by Ralph Waldo Emerson in 1837 in his essay, "The American Scholar," a momentous event in American culture: "The mind of this country, taught to aim at low objects eats upon itself. . . . What is the remedy? . . . We will walk on our own feet . . . we will speak our own minds. The study of letters shall be no longer a name for pity. . . . The dread of man and the love of man shall be a wall of defense and a wreath of joy around all."

Every indication points toward an ever-increasing devotion to the spirit of Emerson's words. The American education explosion, which is probably still in its early stages, is confidently expected by the citizenry to prepare the nation fully for whatever the present requires and the future holds.

A Culture of Diversity

Out of a diversity of peoples, one great nation. Out of a diversity of cultures, one great culture.

Between coast and coast, between Symphony Hall, Boston, and the Los Angeles Music Center for the Performing Arts, between Coney Island and Disneyland, between New York's Lincoln Center and television programs and full-length movies of Hollywood: the American Culture. Then there is the gleeful panorama of Ringling Brothers, Barnum and Bailey, at Madison Square Garden to compare with the lusty winter rodeo at Phoenix, Arizona. Thus, does our American culture currently flourish in all its practical, popular and more permanent forms. Culture, the articulate, sometimes artistic expression of our collective selves.

(Continued on page 127)

Rural church, Iowa.

Mormon Tabernacle, Salt Lake City, Utah.

Harvard's Appleton Chapel, Massachusetts.

Frank Lloyd Wright's Greek Orthodox church, Wauwatosa, Wisconsin.

Church of the Benedictine Priory, St. Louis.

San Xavier del Bac Mission, Arizona.

Illinois Institute of Technology, Chicago.

Cincinnati Contemporary Art Center, Ohio.

Hollywood Bowl, California.

Americans love both the old and new in art, music, drama. Socially-conscious folk singers strum out their plaintive tunes and classical divas of the Metropolitan Opera hit high C, each before commingled audiences, dressed in the heights of fashion or in levis and sandals, either in great halls or at open-air concerts in the magic of a summer night. Over 30,000 have listened to the New York Philharmonic play Stravinsky's *Rite of Spring* in both New York and Milwaukee, and similar performances take place in the old cities of cultural tradition like Boston, Philadelphia, Chicago and in the Western cities of artistic burgeoning like Houston and Denver. And on the West Coast, too, the performing and visual arts richly fill the eyes and ears of thousands in the famous Hollywood Bowl of jet-age Los Angeles and among the once-staid, now beatnik-flecked hills of San Francisco, above the vast and gleaming Golden Gate.

Each year sees the opening of major new cultural centers, music halls, art museums and repertory theatres throughout the country. The acquisition by New York's Metropolitan Museum of Art of Rembrandt's "Aristotle Contemplating a Bust of Homer" in 1961 for over $2 million was major national news and drew hundreds of thousands of people to the museum. A new production at the Tyrone Guthrie Theatre in Minneapolis is of substantial interest in San Francisco and New York.

The impact of American culture abroad is also astounding. The nation that for so long was nurtured in the shadow of mother Europe has now achieved its own eminent place in the world. American musical comedies draw enthusiastic crowds in the capitals of Europe and Asia. The entire world has accepted American jazz as one of the few truly contemporary art forms. American architects such as Frank Lloyd Wright and Edward Durell Stone, modern American writers such as William Faulkner, Ernest Hemingway and John Steinbeck have been given the greatest honors. American symphony orchestras are acknowledged the finest. The Metropolitan Opera and the New York City Ballet are ranked at the top of their realms with only a handful of competitors. Broadway is still one of the world centers of the theatre, Hollywood still unsurpassed as a film capital. American artists, from abstractionist Hans Hofmann to realist Andrew Wyeth to pop artist Andy Warhol, are emulated almost everywhere. On the more popular level of clothes fads and advertising slogans, Europeans complain of the Americanization of Europe.

There is probably no facet of American life during the past 20 years that pleases Americans more than the blooming of their arts. Of course this was by no means a sudden upsurge; it was achieved only after decades of striving. But for those who assume that a nation's arts are indicative of its inner quality, America's cultural explosion is a welcome confirmation.

In the early decades of the Republic the arts were derived from Europe. Most Americans had neither the time nor inclination for the arts. Those who did looked consistently across the Atlantic for guidance and nourishment. American art, architecture and music—except for folk art and folk music, which weren't even considered true art—followed the prevailing European models. Except for the subject matter and setting, the works of Washington Irving, James Fenimore Cooper, Henry Wadsworth Longfellow and even the great Nathaniel Hawthorne could have been written by Englishmen. There is disagreement on the matter, but perhaps it was the poet Walt Whitman who first properly conceived and fulfilled the splendid function of the artist in the American democracy. In the preface to his *Leaves of Grass* in 1855 he did for the arts much what Emerson did for education in his 1837 essay, "The American Scholar," although this certainly influenced the arts too.

Whitman wrote: "The United States themselves are essentially the greatest poem. . . . The proof of a poet is that his country absorbs him as affectionately as he absorbed it." Fifteen years later in *Democratic Vistas* he wrote: "Our fundamental want today in the United States is of a class of native authors. . . ." It was to be many years before many Americans would agree that the arts were fundamental.

Of course Herman Melville's novel, *Moby Dick,* and Henry David Thoreau's *Walden,* are properly American classics, but it was not until

Tyrone Guthrie Theatre,
Minneapolis, Minnesota.

Rehearsal, New York Philharmonic Orchestra.

Mark Twain's *Roughing It* in 1872 and his masterpiece, *The Adventures of Huckleberry Finn*, in 1884, that a truly esteemed American prose voice began to emerge. The culmination of American literature can be said to have come with the awarding of Nobel Prizes for Literature to Sinclair Lewis in 1930, Pearl Buck in 1938, William Faulkner in 1949, Ernest Hemingway in 1954 and John Steinbeck in 1962. Eugene O'Neill, who wrote many fine plays between 1920 and 1956, brought the first world-wide recognition to the American theatre. He and others who followed have been helped by The Theatre Guild, the nation's most influential theatre organization, established in 1919.

The two most original schools of American artists in the 19th century were the Western artists, such as George Catlin and Alfred Jacob Miller, who recorded life beyond the frontier as early as 1832; and the Hudson River School, a term usually applied to a group of artists, including Thomas Cole and Asher B. Durand, who painted landscapes in the northeastern section of the country. Also important was John James Audubon, whose *Birds of America* appeared between 1827 and 1838. Two later masters of American painting whose work remained basically free from European influence were Winslow Homer, whose best work came after the Civil War, and Thomas Eakins, whose objective analysis of the objective world was unsurpassed.

The Armory Show of 1913, organized by a group of painters called "The Eight," was the first major appearance in America of European modernism. Although some esteemed artists, such as Grant Wood and Thomas Hart Benton in the Midwest and Edward Hopper on the East Coast, developed highly representational styles in decades following 1913, it is from the Armory Show that most of the recent trends in American art have emanated. Willem de Kooning, Franz Kline, Jackson Pollock and Mark Tobey, whose styles are either completely abstract or extremely distorted, are only a few

Circular art gallery, Solomon R. Guggenheim Museum, New York.

Door panel by Louis Sullivan, Chicago.

The Rotunda, University of Virginia, Charlottesville.

of the principal artists of mid-century.

The Federal style of architecture was the first to come to prominence after the formation of the Republic. Its foremost achievement was the founding of Washington, D.C., the city plan of which was laid out by the Frenchman Pierre-Charles L'Enfant. The design of the Capitol owes the most to Benjamin Henry Latrobe, the English immigrant who was America's greatest architect in the early 19th century. Thomas Jefferson, an architect in his own right, designed his own superb home, Monticello, and his plans for the University of Virginia created a campus in the 1820's which was unrivaled until Frank Lloyd Wright laid out Florida Southern College in 1940.

The Federal period was followed by the Greek and Gothic Revivals of English origin, the former introduced by Latrobe. The three great monuments to the Gothic Revival are three churches in New York: Trinity, Grace and St. Patrick's; the three were built between 1846 and 1879. The two greatest architects of the late 19th century were H. H. Richardson and Louis Sullivan. One of Richardson's masterpieces was Boston Trinity Church of Romanesque inspiration. It was Richardson's student, Charles F. McKim, who imposed the classic revival on Chicago's World's Fair of 1893. It was in Chicago at about the same time, however, where the foundations were laid for modern American architecture. Louis Sullivan, who believed function and form should be integrated, protested strongly against the classic revival; but he was no slave to functionalism and had a great talent for ornamentation. He was mentor to Frank Lloyd Wright, probably America's greatest architect.

Wright, born in Wisconsin, fought a life-long battle for "organic" architecture. By this he meant a building should be specially designed for, and "grow" naturally from, its site. Among his most famous designs are the Johnson House, Racine, Wisconsin, built in 1937, and the Guggenheim Museum, New York, which was completed in 1959. Among the leading American architects of the mid-20th century are, in addition to Edward Durell Stone, Eero Saarinen, Mies van der Rohe, Philip C. Johnson and Richard J. Neutra.

Wright's designing the Guggenheim Museum is just one example of the important place museums have had in the development of culture in America. The first museum in America was established in Charleston, South Carolina, in 1773. Its first recorded acquisition was a drawing of the head of a bird. From this humble beginning, the nation has accumulated the most impressive array of museums of any country in the world. America's greatest art museums—the Metropolitan in New York, the Museum of Fine Arts in Boston, the National Gallery in Washington, D.C., the Philadelphia Museum, the Art Institute in Chicago—have collections ranking with any in the world. The Smithsonian Institution, although perhaps best known for its scientific and technological exhibits, contains an almost unimaginable range of materials. Fine special museums include the Museum of Science and Industry in Chicago; the Buffalo Bill Museum and Whitney Gallery of Western Art in Cody, Wyoming; the American Museum of Natural History and the

131

Museum of the American Indian, both in New York; the Shelburne Museum of early Americana in Shelburne, Vermont; and the Circus World Museum in Baraboo, Wisconsin.

As important as museums to the development of American culture have been the nation's libraries. The nation's greatest library is the Library of Congress, established by act of Congress in 1800. The original collections of the library, obtained from London, consisted of 152 works in 740 volumes. The functions of the library have been extended by Congress until it is now, in effect, the national library. Today it contains well over 13 million books and pamphlets, growing by 200,000 books and two million items a year. But perhaps the most significant development in the history of American libraries was industrialist Andrew Carnegie's philanthropy. Beginning in the 1880's, Carnegie provided funds for the building of 1,689 libraries in the United States. In each case the municipal government had to provide the site and pass an ordinance for the purchase of books and for future maintenance of the library through taxation. Major libraries, in addition to the Library of Congress, include the New York, Chicago, Cleveland, Philadelphia and Los Angeles Public Libraries and the libraries of Harvard, Yale, Columbia, University of Illinois, University of California at Berkeley and the University of Michigan.

In *Leaves of Grass* Walt Whitman wrote: "I hear America singing, the varied carols I hear," but it was many years after the founding of the nation before America found and recognized its true musical voice. Psalm singing had been an integral part of the Puritans' religious worship. In 1640 they published a collection popularly known as the *Bay Psalm Book*. Those few Americans who have heard this music know its beauty, but unfortunately it remained little known to the rest of the country. The Moravians in Pennsylvania in the early 18th century also had a highly developed religious music of distinction.

The first recorded public concert was in Boston in 1731; Charleston, South Carolina, followed the next year. Several musical societies were founded in the first half of the 19th century, including Boston's Handel and Haydn Society in 1815 and the Musical Fund Society of Philadelphia in 1820. The Philharmonic Society of New York, founded in 1842, has lived to be the oldest permanent orchestra in the country. New Orleans, as early as 1791, was probably the first American city to hear Grand Opera. New York had no continuing opera until the Academy of Music was built in 1854. It was succeeded by the Metropolitan Opera House which opened in 1883. During those decades the great European soloists, such as Jenny Lind, frequently toured the country.

Edward MacDowell, who was born in 1861, was the first American composer who consciously and successfully established an American idiom in classical music. His artistic descendants in the 20th century include Charles Ives, who had to make his living as an insurance executive; Aaron Copland, whose *Appalachian Spring* is one of the few modern American classical pieces played regularly by American orchestras; Samuel Barber, who has written some fine operas; and Virgil Thomson, whose reputation as a critic almost rivals his fame as a composer.

In the latter half of the 19th century, German-born Theodore Thomas' touring orchestra did much to acquaint the American public with fine symphonic music. By the close of that century, many large American cities, such as St. Louis, Boston, Chicago, Cincinnati, Pittsburgh and Philadelphia, had established permanent orchestras. During the years from 1856 to 1868, the New England Conservatory in Boston, the Oberlin Conservatory in Ohio, the Cincinnati Conservatory and the Peabody Conservatory in Baltimore were founded. Despite these and the later establishments of the Eastman School in Rochester, Juilliard School in New York City and the Curtis Institute in Philadelphia, few American classical music performers, instrumental or vocal, were allowed a chance to succeed without substantial training in Europe. Some opera singers even adopted Italian-sounding names. After World War II, however, this began to change, and with pianist Van Cliburn's winning of the prestigious International Tchaikovsky Competition in Russia in 1958 the excellence of strictly American musical training was accepted. When he returned to his native land, in New York he received the first ticker-tape parade ever given a musician.

Today the musical life of America is rich and full.

On the 150th anniversary of Boston's Handel and Haydn Society, in October of 1965, other nationally famous choirs like the Westminster Choir of New Jersey's Westminster Choir College and Pennsylvania's Bethlehem Bach Choir were brought into Symphony Hall for joint and individual concerts. Singers in the Handel and Haydn choir reflect a goodly democracy in that its members — housewives, secretaries, laborers, doctors, lawyers, teachers, people from all walks of life — come from points quite distant from Boston like Portland, Maine; Litchfield, Connecticut and Providence, Rhode Island.

Famed Society conductor, Edward Gilday, preceptor and stimulator of their rich *esprit de corps* characteristically taps his baton against the rostrum and says: "*The Messiah* is an ecclesiastical way of saying 'Hooray for the Lord!' Let your hair down, lose yourself in the anonymity of 150 voices."

In a similar way, one can see an American cultural kinship between the Handel and Haydn group and the great lusty reverence of the Mormon Tabernacle Choir in Salt Lake City, so well-known to millions of national radio and television devotees.

The richness of our classical music culture can be seen in the great tribute paid to American cultural maturity when the Pittsburgh Symphony Orchestra, conducted by William Steinberg, was invited to give a concert at the annual Edinburgh International Festival of Music and Drama in 1965. The United States, in the fall of that same year, was represented in the Madrid Festival by compositions of Aaron Copland, Virgil Thomson, Walter Piston, Gerald Strang and Quincy Porter.

In New York and Boston, the fabled Philharmonic and the Hub's storied

Symphony have become more and more available to the general public. The New York Philharmonic continues to give free summer concerts such as those in the Bronx Botanical Gardens, and the Boston Symphony plays majestically at Tanglewood in the Berkshires, while the Boston Pops group, under the direction of Arthur Fiedler, moves to the Esplanade Shell, along the Charles River, to regale music lovers beneath the summer starlight.

Chicago may be called the cultural stronghold of the Midwest because of its museums, universities, the Civic Opera House — which is distinguished for the presentation of ballet and the Lyric Opera of Chicago — and because of the Chicago Symphony, which performs under the lakeside summer moon at Grant and Ravinia Parks. But it is perhaps the Windy City's "step-fatherhood" of jazz in its northward evolution from New Orleans which has continued to help sustain that city in cultural prominence.

Jazz trumpet.

Jazz brings up the question of popular culture, as distinct from so-called elite culture, in American life. Every civilized society has produced a culture of the classes and a culture of the masses. In America, however, the distinction between the two is blurred because of the traditional fluidity of social position and the more recent phenomenon of the spreading of both kinds of culture by the mass media. This situation has its strengths and weaknesses. The elite arts are more readily available to everyone, but the popular arts absorb the work of even the best playwrights, composers and novelists, sometimes causing a slackening in their discipline. Perhaps both factors have been responsible for the great achievements of Americans in various kinds of popular culture. This is most obvious in those areas, such as jazz, musical comedy and movies, that are coming to be recognized as new, highly developed art forms in their own rights. The popular arts of today sometimes become the elite arts of tomorrow.

The minstrel shows, which became popular in the 1830's and 1840's, were an early example of typically American popular culture. Their black-faced performers sang dialect songs that were by no means Negro folk songs but were definitely American. It was for minstrel shows — which later were to lose their popularity because of their unfair stereotyping of the Negro — that Stephen Foster composed most of his songs, such as "My Old Kentucky Home." "Tin-Pan-Alley," a term applied to 28th Street in New York between Fifth and Broadway from 1900 to after World War I, was the home of popular music publishing houses during the years when their work reached a new height of commercial acceptance. At about this same time, band music was becoming extremely popular, primarily under the impetus of bandmaster-composer John Philip Sousa, who wrote the famous "The Stars and Stripes Forever" march and many others. Beginning in the 1920's the American musical comedy began to replace the European operettas as a source of some of the more durable popular music in this country. Composers and lyricists such as Lorenz Hart, Richard Rodgers, Oscar Hammerstein and Cole Porter became America's most famous and financially successful musicians.

It is jazz, however, that has had the most far-reaching effect on music in America and abroad. The elements of jazz, many of them originating with the Negro, began to synthesize around the turn of the century, particularly in New Orleans. There the basic instrumentation of jazz—cornet or trumpet, trombone, clarinet, bass, banjo or guitar, drums and piano, when not in parades—was developed and there the legendary figures of early jazz—King Oliver, Jelly Roll Morton, Sidney Bechet, Louis "Satchmo" Armstrong and others—performed for 20 or 30 years. In the 1920's jazz migrated northward to Memphis, Kansas City, New York and Chicago. This last city gave its name to a special staccato style of jazz. Jazz gradually made its way into many dance bands and thus began the next development in jazz called "swing." Although much of jazz's improvisational quality was lost, swing reached a high level of popularity in the late 1930's, climaxed by the Benny Goodman concert in venerable Carnegie Hall, heretofore the bastion of classical music. Other successful "big bands" of this era were those of Tommy and Jimmy Dorsey, Glenn Miller, Harry James, Duke Ellington, Count Basie and Artie Shaw.

After World War II, modern jazz developed new concepts, such as the "bop" of trumpeter Dizzy Gillespie and saxophonist Charlie "Bird" Parker, "progressive" jazz played by Stan Kenton and Woody Herman, and the "cool" jazz of Dave Brubeck and the Modern Jazz Quartet. Today these and most of the earlier styles of jazz have become accepted by a broad range of Americans with a major interest in music. Jazz themes and rhythms are even being used in classical forms of music. One of the first composers to do this was George Gershwin, whose *Rhapsody in Blue* of 1924 is one of the most popular pieces ever written in America.

The various jazz festivals around the country draw huge throngs and

Jazz chanteuse Ella Fitzgerald entertains.

scholarly criticism. Chicago, for example, remains hospitable to many types of jazz from "cool" to "tailgate." Three music halls still feature hot jazz as a main course, and "alligators" from all over the nation may be found listening enrapturedly as Dixieland and other kinds of jazz bands pound it out, or as the incomparable jazz singer, Ella Fitzgerald, moans her tragic notes. At places like Jazz Ltd., Dixieland style is a staple with personalities like Bill Reinhardt associated with mastery of the clarinet. James Yancey is familiar as "Dean of Boogie" at the piano, Bobby Hackett is still remembered for an ace trumpet which backed up the blues singing Lee Wiley. Recalled at the Bee Hive is Miff Mole, whose trombone is a landmark in jazz history.

Meanwhile in other cities other kinds of music also prosper. Across the plains from Chicago, in Denver, the symphony makes majestic sounds to majestic backgrounds in Red Rocks and Aspen. Then, too, in the environs of many cities, is the summer music tent, rivaling in stars and quality the long-established "straw hat" theatre circuit.

Over the Great Divide and beside the Western Sea is the giant, well-financed growth of musical culture in Los Angeles. There, in December of 1964, was opened the Pavilion of the Los Angeles Music Center for the Performing Arts. It was the first of three buildings of the project to be erected and is the new home of the Los Angeles Philharmonic Orchestra. That seasoned and highly reputable organization is under the baton of a dynamic young conductor from India, Zubin Mehta.

The initial program is worth noting. It included a fanfare for brass and drums by Richard Strauss; *American Festival Overture* by William Schumann, American composer and president of Lincoln Center for the Performing Arts in New York City; *Feste Romane* by Ottorino Respighi; and Beethoven's *Violin Concerto No. 5*, with Jascha Heifetz as soloist. During the Dedication Week, Mr. Mehta conducted, among other works, Beethoven's *Ninth Symphony* and Stravinsky's *Rite of Spring*.

And other areas of American culture are thriving and growing.

American architecture, for example, reflects and is integral to our culture. Ian McCallum in his *Architecture U.S.A.* maintains that three conditions for great architecture are to be found at their best in the United States: "A prosperous and lively building industry, creative freedom and a conspicuous expenditure." The many modern homes of almost infinite number which are conceived and built with grace, strength and utility are testimonies to this.

Their one principal characteristic seems to be that they invite the outside in. The big picture window is now so familiar that it invites satire. But as a London *Times* commentator put it: "Its openness, its willingness to dispense with privacy, puts it at the opposite extreme from the English house with its walls and its front door without a door knob."

The variety and splendor of our skyscrapers continue to intrigue visitors from other lands. The impact on visitors by New York towers now must be shared by the evocative grace of buildings like those ringing Hartford, Connecticut's imposing Constitution Plaza and cultural landmarks like the

Lincoln Center, New York.

Towers of the University of Pittsburgh and the University of California.

Astute Europeans think that ____ finest and most honest manifestations of our culture are expressed in American literature, particularly in poetry and prose. Our drama, it is said, with considerable truth, reflects "the dark side of the American experience." Tennessee Williams and Arthur Miller, perhaps our leading dramatists, dwell with undeniable eloquence and verisimilitude on themes of frustration and despair, but seldom without some hint of hope.

Much of this, along with the sunshine and light of our musicals, emanates from Broadway, and particularly in the candid Off-Broadway mushrooming, which in the "little theatre" spirit has spread to a kind of repertory, sponsoring independent production companies in many of the cities of our land, far-removed from Broadway and Off-Broadway. One can only be grateful for the more dedicated Off-Broadway people and their influence on repertory and little theatre throughout the nation — and impressed, too, when one considers a set of annual statistics involving their productions.

In one recent season there were a total of 99 productions, of which 64 were premieres, original or new plays not produced before. Of the total, 24 were musicals and 75 complete plays. Almost two million tickets were sold in this recent period and the total cost of production for 99 dramatic projects was $1,845,000. On highly commercial, yet entertaining Broadway itself, with 94 productions (28 musicals and 66 plays) in the same annual season, eight million tickets were sold, with a $7.2 million production cost.

Off-Broadway's tributary value and spontaneous encouragement to little theatres, community drama groups and repertory, in the barns, civic halls, school auditoriums and cities and towns across the land, can be understood, not only in terms of the training of playwrights, producers, actors and technicians—who invariably move out into other communities, forming similar groups—but also in the success of independent action.

The noblest and most accomplished expression of our literature, and indeed our culture, may certainly be found in the lyrical and narrative poems — and indeed in the rustic, wise and philosophical letters and commentary — of the late Robert Frost. He was recently called, while still alive, the "greatest poet writing in English." "His view of life," an English critic wrote, "is Olympian in its wisdom and yet is marked both by sympathy and a sense of sin and evil. The sympathy is there often — in 'The Death of the Hired Man' for example — but sin appears seldom. Yet sin and evil have their place. . . ."

Who can forget his great, snow-capped head and craggy, old-man-of-the-mountain profile as he blinked in the snow-reflected sun at John F. Kennedy's inaugural in 1961. "The land was ours before we were the land's. . . ." he read, as the country watched their greatest poet on nation-wide television.

Our literature, our culture, lost a precious gem of expression when he died.

In symbolic understanding of our culture, perhaps Frost's simple words can be applied collectively to the monumental strivings of our people, in darkness and in light, to show a cultural image of Europe, of the expanded West, of the native American Indian, of the Asian immigration, of all of America's melting pot greatness in this treasured land.

The woods are lovely, dark and deep,
But I have promises to keep,
And miles to go before I sleep . . . .

Times Square theatre district, New York

America is a Miracle of Production and Motion

IV

Colossus of Industry

America is a miracle of industry. From a basically agricultural nation a little over a half-century ago, it has moved to the forefront of the world in technology and advanced industry. Its emergence is a tribute to the viability of the free enterprise system, given a boost where needed and being restrained when necessary by government.

There is a beauty to the sterile shaft of glass that juts out of the skyline of New York, and there is also utility; for the glass shaft that is a skyscraper houses men who keep whirling a portion of the vast industries that gear America for the world-wide leadership that is hers.

Smoke rising from hundreds of smokestacks in Pittsburgh and Gary, Indiana; beer brewing in giant copper kettles in Milwaukee; the glistening, sleek bodies of jetliners on an assembly line in Seattle; towering oil derricks in Texas and mining superstructures in Montana; sprawling, highly automated chemical plants in New Jersey; spacious, clinically clean drug laboratories in Michigan; the sputtering of welding torches in a shipyard in Toledo, Ohio — these are the sights and sounds of American industry.

Industry is a word that is used widely and with many connotations;

Heavy construction workers, Midwest.

but, in its broadest meaning, it includes all those operations which provide us with all the things we need and all the articles we desire in an affluent nation. The growth of industry is predicated upon two basic elements at the outset. One is natural resources, the other is capital, each provided in many forms. Minerals, water power, timber and fertile soil are the natural resources; capital furnishes the money to provide tools, construct machines and build factories which eventually combine to make the huge variety of products that come to the consumer. Of course labor, which includes workers and managers, is a third basic element necessary before natural resources and capital can produce goods.

When Washington became President small businesses, usually family owned, conducted most of the industry in this country, and manufacturing was still in the handicraft stage. Modern small businesses, which play an important part in the American economy, despite the rise of huge corporations, are the inheritors of that early tradition. With the exception of water-powered mills — which were fought by handsawyers who were afraid of losing work — this country's homespun economy before 1790 was powered solely by human muscles and animals.

In 1793, Eli Whitney perfected the cotton gin, the first of a long line of American inventions which have continuously given impetus to the nation's economy. The many interruptions of the flow of imported manufactured products, from the beginning of the Revolution to the end of the War of 1812, created the need for the first factories, such as the same Mr. Whitney's gun factory in Whitneyville, Connecticut.

Between the War of 1812 and the Civil War the basic pattern of American finance, manufacturing and marketing developed. Because of the scarcity of accumulated funds, the corporate organization was devised as a way of assembling capital. The efforts of Whitney and others simplified the operations of manufacturing by the use of standardized, interchangeable parts. This, combined with the introduction of automatic machinery, eventually resulted in the American system of mass production. The Yankee pedlar (who could outwit sales resistance as shrewdly as his Puritan ancestors fooled Satan) was the original salesman and distributor of this new plenitude.

In 1851, America proudly displayed her goods to the world at the Great Exhibition in London. The Centennial Exhibition at Philadelphia in 1876 for the first time enabled Americans to compare foreign and domestic manufacturing achievements. By 1890 the United States had surpassed England and Germany in the volume of iron and steel produced and thus had become the world's leading industrial nation.

The establishment of the Standard Oil Trust, which dominated oil refining by 1882, and the establishment of subsequent trusts, eventually resulted in the Sherman Act of 1890 to prohibit this kind of monopoly. But the nation was growing and so were its businesses. The formation of the United States Steel Corporation in 1901 helped to begin the trends by which control over many big companies passed from large stockholders to investment bankers and management was given over to professional salaried managers.

American inventors continued to play a significant role in the develop-

(Continued on page 147)

San Francisco-Oakland Bay Bridge.

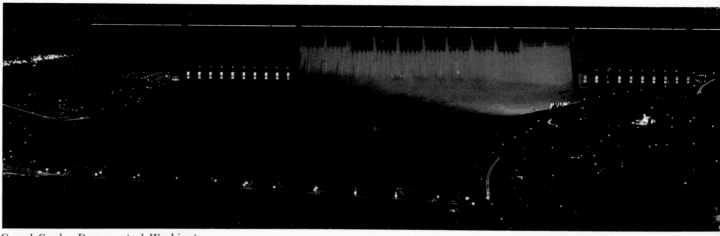
Grand Coulee Dam, central Washington.

St. Paul railroad yards, Minnesota.

Old-fashioned cider press, Kentucky.

Parker Ranch, Hawaii Island.

Mine shafts, western Montana.

San Joaquin Valley orchard, California.

Brewery, Milwaukee, Wisconsin.

Sun touches wheat field, eastern Washington.

ment of the economy, particularly Thomas Alva Edison. One of his inventions was a vote recorder, for which little practical use was found. In 1876 he established the famous laboratory in Menlo Park, New Jersey, where the following year he invented the first practical phonograph. His greatest achievement, however, came in 1879 when he produced the first commercially practical incandescent lamp, using a carbon filament, which ushered in the age of electricity and all its wonders. In 1891 he patented his kinetoscope, a precursor of the motion picture projector, and thus the "genius of the age," as he was called, continued his creativity until a few months before he died in 1931. Three days after his death President Herbert Hoover paid Edison tribute by having millions of Americans turn out their lights to plunge the nation into momentary symbolic darkness.

One of the brilliant innovators of American industry in the 20th century was a slightly built, but intensely determined and opinionated man from Michigan — Henry Ford. He organized the Ford Motor Company shortly after the turn of the century and, like his competitors, at first made automobiles only for the wealthy. But in 1908 he designed the inexpensive Model T so that almost every man could own an automobile, and brought enormous success to his company.

Then in 1914, he attracted nationwide attention with his announcement that he was cutting the work day from nine hours to eight and setting a minimum wage of $5 a day for his employees. He also put forth the then unusual idea that profits should be used to add to the company's factories rather than their going to the stockholders as dividends.

Ford held many seemingly contradictory beliefs, but one that bore fruit for the nation was his support of philanthropic activities. The Ford Foundation, like the earlier established Carnegie and Rockefeller Foundations, has spent millions in bettering almost every worthwhile phase of American life.

Among other important trends in 20th-century American industry were those that particularly came to the fore after World War II: diversification of product lines, relocation of plants outside of old industrial concentrations, increased use of scientific research to develop new products and an increased pace in corporation mergers.

But perhaps there has been nothing more important to America's economic life in this century than the rise of the labor union. Although the first labor strike in the United States was in Philadelphia in 1786 when printers left their jobs to protest a cut in pay below $6 per week, the American labor movement did not really begin to grow until after the Civil War. Individual unions joined together in 1886 to form the American Federation of Labor (A. F. of L.) electing a former cigar maker, Samuel Gompers, as its first president. He was to retain that title for 37 years, leading skilled labor through many crises — strikes and pyrrhic victories, injunctions and ill will — to bring dignity and a better life to the labor force of the United States.

Mass production and oligopolies brought about the industrial union which included all workers in an industry rather than all workers in a skilled category. Thus in 1938 the Congress of Industrial Organizations (C.I.O.)

was formed by mass industrial unions, which elected the fiery and taciturn John Llewellyn Lewis of the United Mine Workers as its first president. The A.F. of L. and the C.I.O. merged in 1955 with A.F. of L. President George Meany as President and C.I.O. and United Auto Workers President Walter Reuther as Vice President. Although strikes and boycotts have been used, the majority of labor's rightful gains have come through cooperation, an attitude attributable to Samuel Gompers, who chose to work with, rather than against, the capitalistic system because he believed it to be a good system.

America today is, by a considerable margin, the leading industrial nation in the world and the trend is still toward even more industrialization. But, so great has the expansion been, that America now faces a new era.

Many feel that automation will open up a far more leisurely and contented life for the entire populace. Workers will work fewer hours, on much more sophisticated machines, and reap the same incomes, with a counter blessing of more recreation time.

The gross national product for the United States in 1965 was $676.3 billion, an increase of $120 billion over 1962 when it was $556.2 billion. That same year, the second most industrialized state, Russia, had a gross national product of $162.4 billion. West Germany and Great Britain ranked third and fourth with totals, respectively, of $90.2 billion and $79.4 billion.

The population of the United States represents approximately six and one-half per cent of the world's people, yet Americans use more than 40 per cent of the world's electrical power, more than 50 per cent of the world's radios, about 50 per cent of the world's telephones, 90 per cent of the world's television sets and more than 50 per cent of the world's motor vehicles.

The American system of industry is based on competitive enterprise, widely termed the private or free enterprise system. Under this system, the man who invents the better system or makes the better product reaps the profits of his own ingenuity. Basically, the American system demands the production of more and more products for private profit, with the result that such increased production shall bring about more widespread distribution of the products, at lower prices and disburse an ever-increasing total volume of wages to more and more people.

This system has its weaknesses and has faltered a few times in the past. It has also been abused. But today this system provides the average American with the highest standard of living in the history of mankind. True, there are pockets of people in this nation to whom the blessings have not yet descended, but presently, an enlightened government and a genuinely concerned industry are sincerely attempting to bring these treasures to this underprivileged fractional minority.

The key to much of this stems from a basic approach of the American citizen to what his government is and what his fellow man has a right to expect. This has been called "social mobility" and what it means is that the American attitude recognizes the right of any man to move from one stratum of society to another if he can do so on the basis of his own talent, drive, discipline and ability.

Despite the enormous fortunes that have accrued to many through the free enterprise system, the basic notion that each man is entitled to what he wants — this side of morality and the law — is endemic to the system. And it is this, with government supervision to eliminate abuses, that has kept the American industrial economy on an almost continual rise, particularly since the World War I era when sharper increases in production began.

Through industry's far-ranging programs of expansion, the dollar value of income per American has far outstripped the contraction of the dollar's value over the past several decades. The nay-sayers' predictions of the collapse of the industrial society in this nation have been proved unfounded again and again; and all predications of the future seem to postulate a continuing expansion.

In the United States there are some four million business and industrial firms, which, under the terms of the broad definition of industry given previously, come under one category.

By far the majority of these comprise what are considered small firms, those which employ relatively few persons. Many are one or two-man operations functioning, in the latter case, as a partnership. Usually, these are the retail firms that distribute the goods to the consumer. At the same time, most corporations in the United States are small businesses, some 550,000 of them coming under that general heading. A family which operates a small food store or a hat shop many times incorporates so there will be no question of having valid licensing powers, in the event that one or another of the partners dies. When we come to industrial ownership in the United States, however, we find that about one-fifth of the total goods and services produced is the result of the efforts of about 50 giant corporations.

Manufacturing accounts for three-fourths of all goods produced in the United States. In fact, American factories manufacture two-fifths of the free world's total industrial production. It is not surprising then that some manufacturing companies have become gigantic. General Motors, for example, one of America's largest corporations, has assets of more than $9.6 billion. Other major companies in various fields include: American Telephone and Telegraph; Texaco; General Foods; United States Steel; Ford Motor Company; E. I. du Pont de Nemours; General Electric; Westinghouse; Goodyear Tire and Rubber; Firestone; Radio Corporation of America; Commonwealth Edison; Pennsylvania and New York Central Railroads; Aluminum Corporation of America; Sears Roebuck; Procter & Gamble; Swift; North American Aviation; and Union Carbide.

The magic of the United States automobile industry probably has touched the minds of more people than any other single element in the fabric of American industry. The availability of automobiles, at price levels within the reach of even a teenage youngster, has hit the imagination of all mankind because possession of an automobile fulfills a desire and an aspiration of the average man everywhere. Henry Ford's idea that everyone should have an automobile has "caught on" throughout the world in a manner and to an extent that is difficult even for Americans to realize.

As the industry has burgeoned, the automobile companies have had to increase the number of outlets to sell the new cars. This has meant expand-

Bank, La Salle Street financial district, Chicago.

ing dealerships across the nation and has also created a need for setting up training schools where dealers learn to sell the product effectively and mechanics can learn how to service it when something goes wrong.

Ford's methods were duplicated by others, and from this, in the true spirit of American capitalism, came the competitive thrusts which turned the manufacturers toward all kinds of communications media in order to detail the better points of their product through advertising.

From these came a whole string of other needs. Men skilled in marketing products were trained to determine which new fields might prove to be worthwhile additions to existing operations; men trained in finance were given special experience with the financing problems of the automobile industry so that their talents could be directed at easing and eliminating them. The list of such new enterprises — totally unrelated in essence to the physical production of automobiles, but now inextricable from it—grows every year.

What took place in the automobile industry occurred, in practically the same order, in other industries. The financial men—who made the decisions on what kind of plant expansion was needed and where best, within a given area, its needs and objectives might most economically be filled—applied their knowledge in many other fields.

This kind of generative process of course brought with it problems that deeply involved the worker. The skilled artisan finds little satisfaction in performing a few monotonous, ever repeated actions which comprise his total contribution to the finished product. The assembly line carries work to the worker so that he does not have to be mobile, but the system also removes the need for him to use his muscles. At the same time, advanced technology has made the skilled worker disturbed over his job future. This kind of worry now is among the problems of automation, and many of the strikes in major industries in the United States today stem directly from this concern. The fact is that the sweeping advances of science have not been matched by equally sweeping efforts to ease their impact upon the worker. These problems have also been compounded by the fact that organized labor groups are hesitant about automation being introduced into their industries for fear of the elimination of many jobs. This is an understandable posture, and labor, government and management are trying to solve it through cooperation, education and retraining.

The new type of industry has created a new "class" — management. In addition to other qualifications, today's executive must be well enough grounded in science to recognize — preferably ahead of his competitors — how the scientific technology can be applied to his own industry. Such is the complexity of today's industry that the knowledge of administrative techniques must be buttressed by a deep awareness of technology, if success is to be achieved. And this is the goal that American education is helping to achieve.

If the United States continues to forge ahead at its present pace, experts indicate that the standard of living could double every 40 years. The next industrial revolution hopefully will lift man from the tedium of the automatic response to a machine's needs. This achievement will be attained in the United States at a breathtaking pace—and, in fact, it is already being accomplished through incredible electronic equipment—such as the computer—that is increasingly becoming a major part of the industrial picture.

These "machines," developed by such companies as International Business Machines, and what they can do, is almost enough to make man fear that he is becoming obsolete. They can figure a million times faster than a man's brain; and they can operate around the clock without any of the fatigue that would beset a man. But—as of now, at least—they cannot replace man because they can only operate on the basis of the "knowledge" man feeds into them. And yet their potential, as projected into the future, is that they will eventually free man's mind for higher levels of thinking, the results of which, in turn, can be incorporated into the machine, thus permitting man to move still higher in an unending cycle.

This concept is staggering, but it should also be joyous, for the benefits that could thereby come to America will be so massive that we, in our land, could be the harbingers of real benefits to all people in all lands everywhere—even those where cottage industries and the backbreaking toil of less advanced machine industries are now the industrial way of life.

Temples of Commerce

All is quiet and serene a few seconds before 9:30 in the morning in the cavernous Board of Trade room in Chicago's La Salle Street district. A number of men in ill-fitting light tan jackets wander a little aimlessly around the floor and up and down the steps to the "pits." On the half-hour a bell rings and mayhem breaks loose. The men begin frantically shouting at the top of their voices, throwing their arms into the air and occasionally lightly striking another man, who might even take a tumble down the steps. A thousand miles away, the New York Stock Exchange has started its busy day in a slightly more sedate manner.

Thus the temples of commerce, an important part of American industry and business, function with the excitement that few, other than Americans, can bring to the fascinating world of finance.

When Alexander Hamilton managed to consolidate and refund the war debts of the Revolutionary War, a need for brokers rapidly arose. For a few years they would meet to buy and sell under an old buttonwood tree on New York's Wall Street; then, in 1792, 24 brokers founded what is now the New York Stock Exchange. It has been one of the keystones of America's growth ever since.

It does not of course buy or sell securities or set their prices. It merely provides an organized market place where member brokers (or agents) can buy and sell stocks and bonds of American and even a few foreign businesses on behalf of the public. The exchange has 1,366 members and 672 member organizations. For a company to have its shares or bonds listed on the "big board," as it is often called, the exchange's rigid listing requirements, as well as the Federal registration requirements of the Securities and Exchange Commission, must be complied with.

Wall Street and Trinity Church, New York.

Brokers bid in commodity trading pit, Chicago Board of Trade.

Of course when a business firm needs to raise money for capital expansion, it does so by the sale of additional stock or bonds by subscription. None of the money changing hands on the stock exchange goes to these firms; it merely goes from one owner of stock to another. The stock exchange is important in making an investor readier to subscribe to a new issue because he knows he has a place to sell his stock when and if he wants to.

The second largest exchange, the American Stock Exchange, also in New York, was formerly called the New York Curb Exchange because many decades ago the predecessors of its member brokers would do their business along the curbs of certain New York streets. There are today a total of 14 exchanges in the United States, spread from Boston to Honolulu.

The Board of Trade in Chicago, like other, smaller boards of trade in this country, is a voluntary trade association which provides a market place for the buying and selling of commodities such as barley, butter, crude oil, tin and wheat. It also weighs and inspects the commodities and supervises the warehouses that store the goods. Two types of trading are carried on there—cash trading, involving actual commodities; and futures trading, which is the buying and selling of contracts for future deliveries of commodities not yet actually ready for market.

Futures trading is carried on in a pit, with each commodity having its own pit. The brokers stand on the rim or steps leading up to the rim of the pit and trade futures, indicating prices and bids by a set of hand signals which they can change with rapid dexterity. They buy or sell futures contracts in order to make a profit in advance of an increase or decline in prices. Some speculators sell contracts on commodities they do not actually have because they believe that they will be able to buy enough of it to fill the contract at a lower price.

The Chicago Board of Trade, founded in 1848, accounts for 90 per cent of the world's trading in futures contracts and does a total volume of business of more than $50 billion annually, while that of the New York Stock Exchange is $73.2 billion.

Another bulwark of finance in America is the banking system. Robert Morris founded the first commercial bank in the United States in 1781, the Bank of North America. The second, the Bank of Massachusetts, was chartered three years later. By 1811 the nation had 88 state-chartered banks. Federal Banks of the United States, established in 1791 and 1816, were relatively short-lived because of the opposition to them by state banks, although the second lasted for 20 years. The lack of an adequate national regulator of bank currency was finally eased in 1863 with the creation of the National Banking System. Among the many far reaching results of this move was to drive most state banks into the National System and to increase the use of checks for business transactions. Another major improvement came in 1913 with the creation of the Federal Reserve System. This consists of 12 regional banks—coordinated by a central board in Washington—which serves as a bank for the banks, doing for them what they do for business firms and individuals.

An example of the growth of the banking system is that in 1964 banks held demand deposits of $136.413 billion, an increase of $19 billion over the amount in 1960. Among the nation's 14,292 banks, some of the largest are the Bank of America centered in California, and the Manufacturers Hanover Trust Co. and the Chase Manhattan and First National City Banks, all of New York.

Perhaps the most spectacular master in the history of American finance was J. Pierpont Morgan, an American businessman in the grand style. Unlike other famous American businessmen, Morgan did not come from humble beginnings. John D. Rockefeller's father had been a pitch man for patent medicines; Andrew Carnegie had been born in a Scottish weaver's cottage. Morgan's father, Junius Spencer Morgan, had been the wealthy head of a financial firm that linked imperial London with industrializing America. From a level-headed, thrifty and methodical boy he grew to be a big bulky man, not handsome, but very responsible looking and with a direct gaze. Although he engaged in some dubious practices in early years, he was essentially a stabilizing and organizing force in American business. He first achieved prominence in 1873 by breaking the monopoly Jay Cooke's syndicate and held on all Federal Government refunding operations. After the failure of Cooke's firm, the Morgan firm dominated Government financing. In 1895 he formed a syndicate which was able to halt the drain of gold reserves from the U.S. Treasury, but his most daring venture was the creation in 1901 of the United States Steel Corporation.

A man of violent likes and dislikes, he cared neither for public opinion nor publicity; but, when investigated by Congress in 1912, he emerged with no loss of personal credit or prestige. A discriminating book and art collector and benefactor of the Metropolitan Museum of Art, to the end of his days he maintained that "the first requisite of credit is character."

The Abundance of Agriculture

The beginning of the American economic miracle was agriculture; and the abundance of its production remains today, along with the "fuels" of finance and research, a basic source of the American economy's strength. America, in its beginnings, was a pastoral land founded on an economy that was almost purely agricultural; the people literally lived off the land, from hand to mouth.

Agriculture was the first American industry. It became such when the first land-owner hired the first man to assist him in tending to the farm

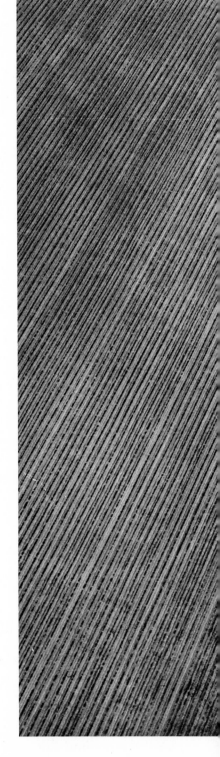

Early cultivation method, horse and plow.

Mechanized planting, Arkansas.

chores. Industry, at its most basic, postulates that an employer-employee relationship—one man hiring another for a salary—implies pay either in produce, in money, by providing shelter, or sometimes all three.

So agriculture is the world's and the nation's oldest industry and it remains the most important, even in a world of massive technological advances. This is true for the simple reason that man must be fed, and in the United States today the food industry, in all its facets, is the nation's biggest business. And yet, because the life of the farmer is difficult, its disciplines rigorous, the returns marginal—particularly at the level of the small farm— the tendency of young people growing up on farms in recent decades has been to flee to the cities and suburbs where the comforts and job opportunities are far more numerous than on the farms. The trend toward the cities began in the early decades of this century, but it was only a trickle then and went unnoticed generally in the face of a political community that was anchored to the rural view of life. Since World War II, however, when the demand for workers in war production plants increased strikingly, the trend toward urban living has accelerated at a tremendous pace.

But agriculture, for all its lack of attraction as a way of life to present-day young people, is still a vital element of the industrial complex of the United States. Even though the small farmer has, in many cases, found it difficult to make a decent living from tilling the soil, the big land holder of farming property has been able to prosper.

Dank cranberry bogs in Massachusetts, Wisconsin and Washington State; waving fields of golden wheat from Ohio through Illinois, Nebraska and the Dakotas to Washington; tall corn from Indiana to Oklahoma; apple orchards in Michigan; peach trees in Georgia; vineyards in California; orange groves in Florida; truck farms in New Jersey and the lower Rio Grande Valley of Texas; handsome dairy cattle in Wisconsin; rugged beef cattle in Kansas, Nebraska and Texas; sheep in Montana and Idaho; the traditional cotton fields in Alabama and Mississippi; tobacco fields covered with white cloth in Connecticut and North Carolina; contoured farmlands in Pennsylvania and Iowa, looking from the air like an abstract painting— all of this gives us only part of the picture of American agriculture today.

Much of this has been brought about by the mechanization of farm work. It began with Cyrus McCormick's Virginia Reaper in 1851, which was displayed in that year at the Great Exposition in London, the first modern world's fair. Its invention was one of the first signs that America was making greater mechanical progress in some areas than Europe. It was also one of the crucial steps in making the United States the world's agricultural leader.

Since then, the hard work that once strained the muscles of the farm laborer and of animals, has largely vanished because of the machines; and, even though the farm worker's day is still a sunup-to-sundown challenge, his actual labor is far easier—just as the discoveries of industrial research have eliminated much of the drudgery for the average housewife in the nation.

In addition, in the field of agronomical research, huge strides have been achieved in bettering the potential yields in all areas of farming. Included are improved seeds, better breeding and feeding practices for livestock, more

155

effective fertilizers for the land and improved methods of irrigation. Among other new products, that are used by masses of Americans, in addition to farmers, are more effective insecticides, pesticides and weed killers.

The final factor which has been massively effective in changing the farm picture in America has been education. A widespread network of extension service centers, which have as their chief purpose the education of the farmer in the use of modern principles and methods, have made living fact of much that was mere unpracticed theory only a few decades back.

A few statistics underscore all of this. For instance, the average yield per acre in the 1950's was more than a third higher than at the turn of the century. Similarly, during the first half of the century, farm production in crops and livestock doubled, while the number of acres cultivated and the farming labor force dropped by one-third.

The skyrocketing output has, however, created problems of distribution and sale. The American farmer produces much more each year than can feasibly be sold at a profit, and, rather than glut the market with produce for which the farmer would receive no profit — would, in fact lose money — the Federal Government has devised various methods for easing the situation.

One of these is the system whereby the Government purchases large amounts of basic crops, such as wheat, and stores them. Under another system farmers are paid a certain amount for *not* planting a percentage of their acreage, thereby eliminating the possibility of oversupply on the market.

In much of the world, farming is still at the subsistence level. This means that the farmer works his land in order to provide only for his family's support. In America, however, the situation is quite different. In the United States two-thirds of the farmers are commercial farmers. These are the men with large holdings, who hire a large number of workers, whose farms are equipped with the most modern machinery and who market almost the entire crop of whatever is raised — cattle, corn, wheat and the like.

The astonishing fact about this is that the commercial farmers, although they represent only two-thirds of the farmers in the nation, are responsible for an estimated 97 per cent of the country's total agricultural production. These figures underscore the enormous revolution in farming methods that has taken place in the United States, whereby the old family farm now plays a smaller part in overall volume of production, but still provides many Americans with an economically adequate and generally satisfying life.

Due to the kind of land available and the amounts of acreage open to farming, the United States can be divided up into areas where one specific kind of farming is the basis of the agricultural economy.

Farming in New England, New York and Pennsylvania, along with Michigan, Wisconsin and Minnesota tends to center around dairy products; the Southeast, excepting Florida, and stretching across to Oklahoma and a large section of northeastern Texas, is cotton country; this belt, and especially those states that hug the Gulf of Mexico, is also a truck farming area — fruits, vegetables and other special products — and truck farming appears in many small areas throughout the nation (cranberries on Cape Cod in Massachusetts, for instance), but especially in California, where the rich soil and steady, warm climate in the valleys make it enormously profitable, particularly for items such as oranges, lemons, dates, grapes, avocados and the like, which need a Mediterranean type of climate, unavailable in the rest of the country except southern Florida. Livestock and feed-grain farming flourishes on the parklands and prairies, and west to the Rockies. It now crops up again on the Pacific side of the mountains. Omaha is now the meat-packing capital of the country.

General or unspecialized farming, is centered along the Ohio Valley and those states bordering the Mississippi where the Ohio empties into it. Wheat and small-grains farming is centered principally in the plains states. However, this geographical outline can be misleading. A specialized farm is one in which over 50 per cent of the produce is of one kind and there are few farms now limited to one crop or product. Nor is any one region limited to any one kind of farming.

In the corn belt — the level, fertile area that extends east and west from the Mississippi in the heartland of the nation — the farmers also cultivate soybeans, oats, wheat, various other "grasses" and vegetables. This system involves crop rotation, whereby a field planted for one product one year is planted with another the following year — again, a practical method of maintaining the fertility of the soil.

Agriculture, despite its primacy among American industries in terms of numbers employed and of total assets, ranks far behind the top income industries in the nation — at least according to the 1965 figures of the Department of Commerce. These figures show that agriculture, combined with forestry and fisheries, comprised an income of almost $20 billion dollars. The corresponding figure for manufacturing was $171.2 billion, while both durable and nondurable goods far surpassed agriculture — the former being $104.6 billion, the latter $66.5 billion. In fact, agriculture stood lowest on the list, the closest being transportation at $23 billion, and communications and public utilities at the same figure. America's food industry, of course, includes much in addition to agriculture. Those who handle the products of agriculture have deliberately devised their operations to bring almost everything that can be grown anywhere in the nation at any time of the year to any consumer throughout the year. All manner of research and ingenuity has gone into this phase of the food industry — that is, the transporting of produce from the farm to the consumer's table by any means.

At one time, along the northern New England coast, there was a crustacean much admired for its delicious taste by gourmets and gourmands alike. It is still there; but, after being greatly reduced in numbers, it is now once again available to restaurants throughout the nation due to "lobster farms," new marketing methods and rapid air transport. This is the path of progress that has been carried out by the modern transportation industry, particularly in recent years through air freight.

The lobster is now taken from the "pond," packed into something such as dry ice and winged to any spot on the globe in a relatively few hours. Similarly, all manner of other specialties from other areas of the nation have been made available rapidly to the nation as a whole. Grapefruit, oranges, avocados and much other warm-climate produce of Florida and California is now marketed in Maine or Oregon within hours. And the pineapple that grows so richly in our 50th state of Hawaii is now only a few flight hours away from markets everywhere in the United States.

Food processing is a major phase of marketing. The miracles wrought by the freezing processes—whereby peas grown in the South, for instance, can be quick-frozen and sold to the housewife in the North who merely tosses them into boiling water for a few minutes to cook—have become commonplace in the past two decades. The period is long past when the staples of the winter, such as potatoes and turnips, were tossed into a cool cellar and then brought out as needed, and peas, beans and tomatoes were summer delights only.

Food packaging, too, has made an enormous contribution to the American food industry. Pre-prepared foods are readily available at any supermarket today. There are pizzas, for example, all rolled out and garnished with sauce, ready for the housewife to toss into her oven for a few minutes to provide what once was a delicacy unknown outside of one tiny village in southern Italy. The number and range of such items includes almost every known kind of food and every type of cuisine. Newburg sauce, once available only at the great restaurants or from the hands of a fine cook at home, can now be picked up in a jar at a market. More recently has come the tremendous effort to market a huge line of dietetic products that are without the sugar content, while maintaining the taste value, which weight-conscious Americans increasingly seek for regular consumption.

The culmination of the food industry, as far as the consumer is concerned, is in most cases the supermarket. The supermarket idea began to develop in the 1930's and expanded greatly after World War II. Food-store chains, such as the Great Atlantic & Pacific Tea Company, today the nation's largest, have capitalized on this concept that is spreading around the world as an efficient means of low-cost food distribution.

Verrazano-Narrows Bridge, New York.

All of this is merely an indication of the kind of practical know-how that has made the American effort and spirit in industry a byword throughout the world. The food industry is merely one of the most familiar, although little appreciated, areas of industrial America. We see the results of it all, but rarely do we stop to ponder its real meaning and true value.

A Nation of Builders

Shelter, like food, is one of life's basic necessities, but in America, as nowhere else on earth, the construction of buildings and other structures has gone far beyond mere necessity. From the archetypical log cabins and sod huts of the pioneer tradition, through the ante-bellum mansions of the South, the adobe ranches of the Southwest and the Victorian gingerbread dwellings of the North, to today's split-levels, the building of houses in this country has grown into a mammoth business.

The building of larger commercial and public edifices and other kinds of construction shows an equally impressive record. John A. Roebling, who immigrated from Germany in 1831, built the country's first suspension bridge, the Brooklyn Bridge, which was completed in 1883. This established the use of steel wire for suspension bridge cables. So, although the first modern suspension bridges were built in Europe, the United States gradually took the lead in long-span suspension bridge design with the Golden Gate Bridge in San Francisco; the George Washington Bridge between New York and New Jersey; the San Francisco-Oakland Bay Bridge; the Mackinac Bridge connecting Michigan's Upper Peninsula with the rest of the state, and finally the Verrazano-Narrows Bridge, the largest suspension bridge in the world, with a center span of 4,260 feet or over three-quarters of a mile, which links Brooklyn with Staten Island, in New York. These enormous giants are triumphs of engineering skill and beauty, and a tribute to the inhabitants' industry and initiative in responding to this country's great natural barriers and to their ability to overcome them with great works.

Other notable accomplishments of American engineering and construction are the Panama Canal, and many magnificent skyscrapers and dams. The first true skyscraper was the Home Insurance Building in Chicago, which was designed by William Le Baron Jenney and completed in 1885. With the 792-foot Woolworth Building of 1911-1913 New York took the lead in skyscrapers, a lead which it has never relinquished. New York's skyscrapers were crowned with the 1,250-foot high Empire State Building of 1930-1931. Overcoming massive engineering problems, the Panama Canal, opened in 1914, was constructed by a 30,000-man force of many nationalities under the masterful direction of George Washington Goethals. The invention of the arch dam in the United States made possible in 1936 the building of the Hoover Dam between Arizona and Nevada; other outstanding dams are the Shasta Dam in California, the Grand Coulee Dam in Washington State and more recent the Glen Canyon Dam in Arizona.

In the United States today there are over three million people earning their living in the building and construction industry. Many of course are

Family scene, restaurant, Chicago.

159

Constitution Plaza skyscrapers, Hartford, Connecticut.

S.S. United States *arrives at Hudson River pier, New York.*

Overseas highway, Florida Keys.

engaged in the seemingly constant rebuilding of American cities that is particularly noticeable in New York City. The largest of these projects is the construction of the Port of New York Authority's World Trade Center. When completed in 1970 its twin 110-story towers, the tallest in the world, will have cost about $525 million. Recent and current projects in other cities include Boston's $150 million Prudential Center, completed in 1965, and Chicago's 100-story John Hancock Center, which is to be completed in 1968, and, with an area of 2.3 million square feet, will be the world's largest combination office-and-apartment building.

The building of private homes, however, remains the major part of the building industry. In housebuilding, as in so many other areas of American commercial enterprise, a simpler technique for doing a complex job was developed in this country in the middle of the 19th century. For centuries men had framed their wooden buildings with heavy timbers that were mortised, tenoned and pegged together and then raised into position by group labor. Of course in many areas of 19th-century America the necessary knowledge for even this procedure was not available. So, in most cases, a makeshift method called "balloon framing" was adopted. Balloon framing was made possible by machine-made nails, which were generally available by the 1830's. The balloon frame consisted of light, two-by-four studs, nailed, rather than joined, in a basket-like manner and rising continuously from foundation to rafters. This fragile-looking skeleton was actually quite strong and, what was at first considered makeshift, became a permanent way of doing things; and it spread throughout the country. Without this labor-saving method the cities from Chicago west would never have grown as rapidly as they did.

The next big housing boom came after World War II, when new techniques, such as the prefabricated home, and new ideas, such as the housing project, enabled builders to keep pace with the enormous demand for living quarters. During the 1950's and early 1960's Americans built over a million new homes per year. The American predilection for each family to own its own home is being satisfied by American enterprise, by the development of savings and loan associations and by the creation of the Federal Housing Administration, founded in 1934 to establish amortized mortgages—a type of mortgage that can be repaid in regular monthly installments rather than in a lump sum. By the 1960's about 62 per cent of American families owned their own homes.

Binding the Nation Together

In a nation as large and diversified as America, it was inevitable that transportation and communications would come to play an especially vital role. This, combined with the American genius for organization, invention and production, has given this country a level of achievement in this field that is envied by all the nations of the world.

Outstanding examples of transportation ingenuity can be seen throughout the country: The seemingly endless plains of concrete freeways in and around Los Angeles; the soaring excitement of airports such as O'Hare in Chicago, John F. Kennedy on Long Island and John Foster Dulles outside of Washington, D. C.; the extensive subway systems of New York and Chicago; New York's huge and almost legendary Grand General Station; the magnificent, proud, new ships of the United States Lines, such as the *S.S. United States;* and, probably the most impressive of all — the Federal Interstate Highway System of multiple-lane, limited-access roads that now connect most of the country's major metropolitan areas.

These great accomplishments have come from humble beginnings. Despite the development of the application of steam to industry in Britain in the late 18th century, America continued to use water power to turn most of the wheels of industry until after the Civil War. Typically, in America, the steam engine was at first used for increased mobility by adapting it to the boat. The steamboat meant unity to the sprawling, young nation to a degree that is difficult to overestimate.

There had been steamboats devised in this country before Robert Fulton ran his *Clermont* up the Hudson River in 1807, but Fulton's success initiated the beginning of the steamboat era in this country. Fulton's double paddle-wheeled boat was America's first important contribution to the Industrial Revolution.

In overland transportation, the Cumberland Road, which stretched from Cumberland, Maryland, to Wheeling, West Virginia, was completed in 1818, and became the main artery for settlers and high-value merchandise heading west. Most Western products, however, were too bulky to be transported overland to the East. But here the steamboat made it possible for the Mississippi River to be developed into a two-way delivery system. The Great Lakes, as an artery of transportation, developed more slowly.

The opening of the Erie Canal in 1825 changed the main flow of traffic in the United States from north-south to east-west. This created an inexpensive water link from the Hudson River to Lake Erie and the entire Mississippi River Valley and insured the predominance of New York City as a commercial center. The success of the Erie Canal caused other areas to build canals, but they only worked where topographical conditions were right and enough water was available.

The full impact of railroads was not felt until after the Civil War, but they began to spread after the completion of the first line, the Baltimore and Ohio, in 1830. The railroad reached the Mississippi in 1854, but it wasn't until 15 years later that construction crews working from the west and the east met and joined tracks of the Central Pacific and Union Pacific at Promontory, Utah. A ceremony was held for the driving of a golden spike to complete the junction, and there was jubilation throughout the nation as the telegraph clicked out the message: "The last rail is laid . . . the last spike driven. . . . The Pacific Railroad is completed."

The progress of the railroad in the 19th century was greatly aided by Federal Government grants of alternate sections of vacant public land to railroads for their road beds, resulting in an alternating checkerboard pattern of private and government land ownership. These grants-in-aid followed

(Continued on page 167)

Floating logs, Washington.

Steel mills, Gary, Indiana.

Kaiser Steel Mill, southern California.

Turkey farm, southern Wisconsin.

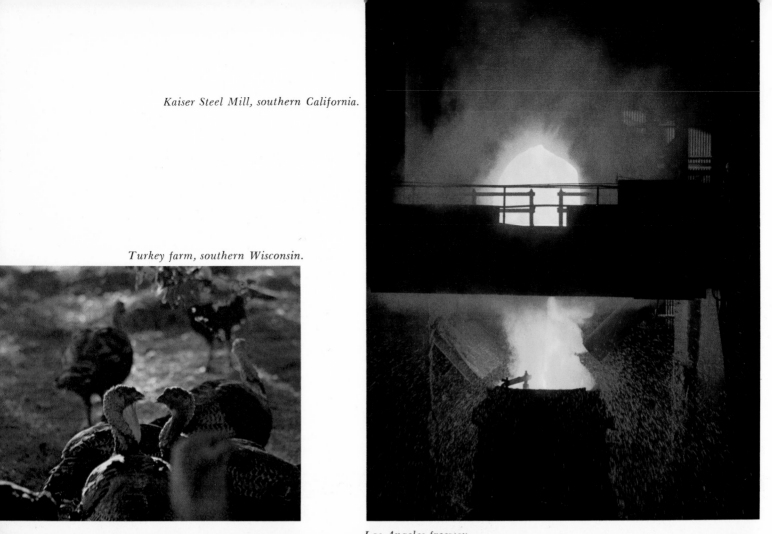

Los Angeles freeway.

U.S. Highway 40, Kansas

Boeing 727, final assembly, Washington.

Contoured farmland, eastern Pennsylvania.

Grain elevator, eastern Nebraska.

Steer, eastern Tennessee.

Union Stock Yards, Omaha, Nebraska.

an earlier precedent of such grants for canals and wagon roads. In the 20th century the practice was continued when the Federal Government provided much of the money for building airports, establishing airlines and building interstate highways.

The years between the Civil War and World War I were those of the greatest growth for the railroads. After 1914, although the railroads remained the principal carriers of goods, they had to share much of the business with other kinds of carriers. There were two main challengers — the pipelines, for carrying gas and liquid fuels; and the trucks. In 1900 there were no trucks recorded in the nation; 50 years later there were 7.8 million registered.

An even bigger change in 20th-century transportation was in the carrying of passengers. The automobile and the airplane have taken most passengers away from the railroads. Today about 50 domestic airlines carry more than 77 million passengers each year; and the highway system covers more than 3.5 million miles and is used by over 80 million vehicles. By the end of 1965 half of the 41,000-mile National System of Interstate and Defense Highways was open to traffic. This program, begun in 1956, is to be completed by 1972 with the Federal Government paying 90 per cent of the cost.

Even today, however, many goods are transported along the nation's remarkable network of inland waterways. Ocean-going ships enter the St. Lawrence River and, by using the jointly built Canadian and United States St. Lawrence Seaway, they can sail to Duluth, Minnesota, at the western end of Lake Superior; or, by entering the Chicago River and Chicago Sanitary and Ship Canal, reach the Mississippi River and the Gulf of Mexico.

An American painter, Samuel F. B. Morse, developed the first practical telegraph instrument in the 1830's after several years of hard work and poverty. It was the first technical means of communication used in the United States when, in 1844, it carried the news to Washington, D. C., of Henry Clay's nomination for President by the Whigs in Baltimore. About three weeks later the line from Washington to Baltimore was formally opened with Morse in the capital sending the message, "What hath God wrought."

American inventors continued to play a significant role in the development of the economy. In 1871 Scots-born Alexander Graham Bell was giving special instruction in various Eastern American cities to teachers of deaf children in the use of his father's physiological symbols of visible speech. Five years later he sent the first sentence ever transmitted by electricity over wires. In addition to all else it provided, the telephone was undoubtedly a major factor in the increase in the total volume of business operations in all the years that have followed. It was not that it increased production efficiency so much as it was that, in the tradition of fierce competition in American business, every businessman found the new gadget necessary as soon as his competitor got one. Today Americans make almost 300 million telephone calls a day over 370 million miles of wires.

Radio and television have each shown tremendous growth since the first scheduled radio programs in the early 1920's and have become an intrinsic

Explorer X satellite launching, Cape Kennedy, Florida.

Los Angeles International Airport, California.

Heavy freight truck, interstate highway, Midwest.

part of the culture that is America. Radio grew rapidly, broadcasting coast-to-coast network programs by 1927, one year after the National Broadcasting Company (NBC) was formed. With increased radio sales, programs such as "Fibber McGee and Molly," "Amos 'n' Andy" and "Death Valley Days" began their long careers in the 1920's and early 1930's. Radio proved its effectiveness when Orson Welles broadcast in 1938 a description of an imaginary Martian invasion and panicked almost the entire Eastern Seaboard.

In World War II, CBS radio news, broadcasting direct from the fronts of the world, brought such news commentators as Edward R. Murrow and H. V. Kaltenborn into prominence. After the war, commercial television began its spectacular climb to the point that today over 90 per cent of the nation has access to television. Radio has changed its live entertainment format to a music-and-news formula, often broadcasting 24 hours a day.

Although radio and television are primarily entertainment media, Franklin D. Roosevelt's "Fireside Chats" on radio in the 1930's set the stage for live broadcasting of political conventions and the first television debate between Presidential candidates in 1960 when 70 million people watched John F. Kennedy and Richard M. Nixon. Television also allowed Americans and much of the world to feel the full impact of the tragedy of the assassination of President Kennedy in November 1963, when all three networks combined their news coverage and eliminated commercial broadcasting for the entire weekend.

It was in television that America recently achieved the latest in her long line of technical triumphs. On June 28, 1965, the first commercial transmission of live television between continents took place. Signals were relayed to Europe from the "Early Bird" satellite, 22,300 miles above the Atlantic Ocean. Early Bird, although owned by a consortium of 47 nations, was primarily constructed, launched and operated under the direction of the privately owned, Government-sponsored Communications Satellite Corporation of the United States.

Newspapers, magazines and books make up another kind of combined entertainment-and-information communications media. Almost 2,000 daily newspapers, 9,000 weeklies, 17,000 magazines and 25,000 new books and new editions yearly are published in the United States. Although in recent years the high cost of production has caused the number of daily papers to decrease, newspaper publishers print about 59 million copies daily. The crucial part played by newspapers, free from any government censorship, in informing the people of this democracy continues to be carried out in the strong tradition of great American newspapermen from the past—such as Horace Greeley, James Gordon Bennett, Joseph Pulitzer, William Randolph Hearst and Colonel Robert McCormick. Today's publishers are perhaps not as controversial as their predecessors, but they are no less dedicated to the vital purpose of their profession.

The communications media have also made invaluable contributions to this country's productivity—specifically, by helping to develop markets for products through advertising; generally, by providing information of all kinds so that Americans can better enjoy the good life that is theirs.

Main street, small Midwestern town.

V | The American Community

The Small Town and Suburban America: Where America Lives

A city today is somehow only as vital as its surroundings, for without them it could not survive. The bankers and breadmakers, the financiers and janitors and the lawyers and laborers may not share the same income bracket but they do have one common ground; a home away from the urban area.

Before the outbreak of World War II, a city was a well-defined area, as self-sufficient and sustaining as the small communities which surrounded it and, save for a few exceptions, were equally dependent upon themselves. The small town people were just that; residents of lovely old and stately homes lining tree-shaded streets with a neighborhood store perhaps only a short walk away. The towns never seemed to change much, and a yellowed photograph taken in 1910, was, except for the size of the trees and perhaps the presence of an automobile, identical with that taken in 1940.

The war brought changes, but they were generally few and unimportant. There was an air raid warden who may have been the hardware store owner wearing a helmet, marching down deserted streets and seeking a hint of light around the ugly black curtains which graced nearly every home in the days of blackouts. There was less traffic because of gasoline rationing, and that small neighborhood store began to feel the pinch of not having enough meat to sell.

Then with a resounding boom heard across the nation the sequestered bubble of Small Town, U.S.A., burst and there was near-chaos as new faces appeared in gaily painted homes erected within months upon what was once

Contemporary suburban home, New York.

Apartment house pattern, South San Francisco.

a farmer's pasture or a country woodlot where children played. The move to suburbia had begun, and not another war nor a recession nor increased taxes could cast sand under the racing wheels bent on deserting the cities.

The veterans came in droves, inhabiting the new homes paid for with mortgages guaranteed by a government grateful for their wartime services. And, as suddenly, the sleepy-appearing brick school was filled to overflowing with children and they took turns attending classes, some in the morning and the other half in the afternoon. New teachers were hired at the rate of one or two for every mile the water and sewer pipes were extended. New schools were built, and the curriculum was upgraded to satisfy the younger and new residents demanding an education for their children equal to that of the city they left a few years before.

The automobile and the joy of owning more than a view of another apartment house has changed the living of America and brought a whole new vocabulary to its language.

The metropolitan area is a sprawl of homes emanating like the rings of Saturn around a planet, or the core city. But there is no astrophysical parallel to metropolitan areas, for they grow and grow without end. It is not inconceivable that nearly all the continental United States will be one enormous metropolitan area a century or so hence. Two-thirds of America lives in these metropolitan areas. Forty of every 100 workers in Chicago choose to live beyond the city, and some 60 per cent of day-time inhabitants of Los Angeles sleep elsewhere.

New Yorkers by day embark on public transportation at dusk and head for Connecticut communities. An astonishing number of license plates seen on automobiles in Boston bear the names of New Hampshire, Rhode Island, Maine and occasionally Connecticut. The area from Portland, Maine, all the way to Washington, D.C., on a direct, shoreline route, contains relatively few open areas among the many cities and towns, all connected with massive bridges, tunnels and superhighways.

There are problems in the metropolitan areas, and not the least of them is the preponderance of government. In the 225-odd metropolitan areas from coast to coast there are more than 18,000 local governmental units. There are 300 counties in them, 2,500 townships, 4,100 municipalities, 5,400 special districts such as public water and sewer units and 6,000 school districts.

All this has brought new hurdles to the outlying areas. Residents of the former pastures, woodlots and forests beg for services equal to those of the cities they recently left. The still-reluctant communities generally fend for themselves, handling their affairs as if they were still an isolated and self-dependent town. Cooperation exists between many, but there is still a long road for others to travel before their affairs and decisions are handled with an eye beyond their own borders. The whole and unpredicted concept of America working in one place and living in another is somehow too new for immediate and completely workable plans for effectiveness.

Planning councils are being formulated by many states to meet head-on

Home scene, Ozark community, Missouri.

the difficulties facing communities which have grown faster than their capabilities could match. They frequently seek a unity of governments, or at least dialogue between the bodies which govern the communities. Services are often a major part of these metropolitan area planning councils attempting to bring to the people a just return for their tax dollar. The services, such as better roads, a more comprehensive education program, new schools, sewerage, street lights and water, are usually furnished on a local level rather than by the Federal Government.

Because of these problems and many others, suburbia has joined American education and the cities as favorite targets for criticism from the citizenry. But its truly remarkable qualities outweigh its problems. The suburbs have become the primary focus and cutting edge of America's daily life, and the generally recognized strength and *elan* of the society as a whole to a considerable extent must be attributed to the suburbs and its inhabitants.

There are all kinds of suburbs. The closely packed, look-alike, jerry-built houses make up only a small minority. For the most part, America's suburban homes show a range of individuality and taste commensurate with the limits of income, setting and building techniques available. The activities of its people, particularly its women, are dazzling: homes charmingly and inventively decorated; a wide variety of elaborately prepared meals, suitable to gourmet tastes; much welfare and charity work; startling accomplishments in the crafts, ranging from rug weaving to glass blowing; excellent gardens of flowers and vegetables, almost always self-maintained; and cultural activities in abundance — for it was in the suburbs that the nation's cultural explosion began. Perhaps some of this is meaningless and superficial, but what nation can rival the ultimate result for which the suburb is substantially responsible — America's greatness, truly the fruit of its people rather than of an elite.

But if the suburb carries the thrust of contemporaneity in America, the small town retains an important place. The nurturing place of Abraham Lincoln and William Faulkner and Lyndon Johnson no longer gives the appearance of being uneventful or static. It still provides a sense of permanence, but not permanence without change. This permanence is the town's strength and comes from its citizenry whose stability, resourcefulness and individuality prevail. It continues to be a place for those who, with Thoreau, want to live more deliberately. At the same time its provincialism has dissipated with the easy communication provided by roads, telephone, radio and television. And it is no longer as certain, as it was in the decade and a half following World War II, that the small town is destined to lose all her most talented sons and daughters. Some stay, some return and some, who cannot, would like to come back.

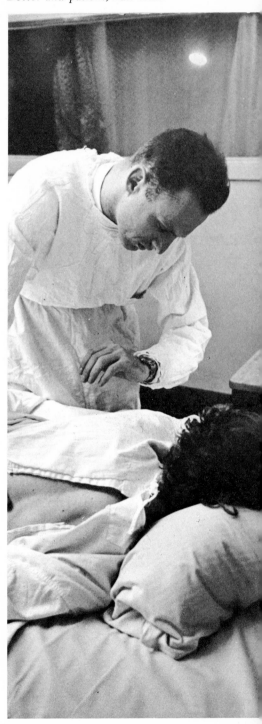

Doctor and patient, East coast.

There are still small towns well-sprinkled across the United States, and a few days spent in one reveals the magnetism they exert on their residents.

Throughout New England are such communities, each separated by miles of roads winding through mountains and past forests and ponds. They are on the fringe or beyond the metropolitan areas, quite self-sufficient in a 20th century manner. Their charm is instantly apparent. There is a village green, or common, holding the shadow of a stately church's steeple. A rambling stone wall laced with honeysuckle and morning glories embraces a cemetery older than the Declaration of Independence. Gleaming white stones, often elaborately incised and decorated, spring from this peaceful place, their inscriptions barely legible after more than two centuries of defying wind, rain and snow.

In the central square of a small town in the South there will be a monument of the rich, gray granite native to the region. It is a Confederate soldier with a sad and tired face, his gnarled hand holding a musket as his sightless eyes gaze to the North. Beneath are the names of the young men of this town who left their farms in 1861 to fight a bitter war, and the names are often still familiar, for their ancestors settled the town and their descendants remain. People know their fellow townsmen and know them well. There are few secrets in a small town or village. If sadness or joy visits a home here the neighbors soon follow, holding out a hand of assistance or congratulation.

In the Midwestern town, there will probably be a new processing plant or two, less than five years old, but on its streets will still be seen those who are farmers despite the decrease in the number of family farms; and chances are they are prosperous and happy in the satisfaction of having wrested a good living from the land with their own hands. The air is filled, not with smoke, but with the perfume of a newly mown hay crop, and the delicate smell of wildflowers is almost everywhere.

The town has its services, and the postmaster, the mailman in his red, white and blue truck and the proprietor of the one store which has a little of everything to offer are on a first-name basis with all. There are church suppers held around long plank tables bent with the weight of homemade breads and hams and preserves. Baseball games attract a heavy crowd on Saturday afternoons in the almost-level field behind the cemetery, and neighbors still

Snow trails and skiers, Minnesota.

visit on Saturday evenings or Sunday afternoons.

These people live here because they want to. Theirs is a love affair with place and time and tempo. It is they and their ancestors, unlike the inhabitants of the villages of Europe, who have played an essential role in the building of their nation. European culture and history is dominated by its capitals; the United States to a large extent evolved from its Lexingtons, Concords, Mount Vernons and Sauk Centers.

America at Play

America has always been a sports-loving nation.

The first men off the Mayflower probably took a utilitarian dip in Cape Cod Bay and presaged the popularity of that body of water as a resort area. Much that was utilitarian in the development of the nation gave birth to sports; for play, to Americans, has always been an integral part of our way of life.

Utilitarian ox teams on their days off were pitted against one another in tugs-of-war. The development of our ocean trade brought forth the clipper ship races, the America's Cup Race and, ultimately a wide range of water sports from canoeing to yachting, from boat racing to water skiing, and from just plain swimming to surfing. The increasing popularity of skin diving traces its origin to the business of professional deep sea diving for exploration and salvage and to the American invention of the submarine. Even the "winning of the West" was not all serious business. From the hard-driving cattle trade developed the rodeo, with its riding and roping for competition and relaxation.

Early in our history, man's tools against the wilderness were often only his hands and his rod and gun. In his rare leisure time he used his hands for wrestling, sometimes Indian style, more often in the classic forms indulged in by such confirmed heroes as Sam Houston and Abe Lincoln. With his rod and gun he turned the utilitarian business of getting food on the table into the sports that made a name for Annie Oakley and brought us the modern pleasure-time pursuits of trap, skeet and target shooting; hunting and fishing.

The utilitarian peach baskets of the growing fruit industry, when nailed high on gymnasium walls, became essential props for James Naismith's invention of basketball in 1891.

Nearly every development in the transportation industry brought a counterpart sport. The invention of the steamboat led to the great Mississippi River paddle-wheel boat races, ancestors of today's race for the blue ribbon that represents the fastest transoceanic passenger ship time to Europe. Railroad locomotives and entire trains vied for the best time to a specified finish line. With the invention of the internal combustion engine another score of sports activities got their start; auto races, transcontinental dashes, endurance contests, rallies; then races for airplane and auto speed records of distances as short as a measured mile or as long as around the world. Competitive Americans continue to seek challenges, and even now, (though probably only for a while) our goal is to be first on the moon.

The story of America at play is also the story of American creativity. New games have been created; games that are totally American, although sometimes deriving from other sports. Baseball finds its origins in English rounders; football in British rugby. The American games are now completely stylized however, and no self-respecting rounders or rugby fan would see the faintest resemblance in these off-shoot sports.

Although baseball is called "the national pastime," the average amateur player is hard put to get together seventeen others and locate a regulation-size baseball field. Hence the development of softball. The softer ball used provides a margin of safety; the smaller playing field makes the real estate search simpler. Another growing offspring of standard baseball is Little League baseball, which even has its own hard-fought world series each year in Williamsport, Pennsylvania. Teams of young boys from all over the United States, and from as far away as Japan, compete in the scaled-down sport.

Golf, which did not originate in this country, has had many offshoots here; miniature golf, pitch and putt, putting greens, driving ranges and even hole-in-one tournaments. The combination of golf's outdoor activity and individual skill have increased its popularity across the nation.

Football has not been innocent of adaptation either. Just as rugby begat football, it begat touch football and five-man football.

Touch football was a game dear to the hearts of the late President John F. Kennedy, his family and friends and was played on the White House grounds. Around the Kennedys' interest in athletics was formed the President's Physical Fitness Program, with its emphasis on participation in sports, not merely watching them.

Said the President: "We do not want in the United States a nation of spectators. We want a nation of participants in the vigorous life. This is not a matter which can be settled, of course, from Washington. It is really a matter which starts with each individual family. It is my hope that mothers and fathers, stretching across the United States, will be concerned about this phase of their children's development, that the communities will be concerned, to make it possible for young boys and girls to participate actively in the physical life; and that men and women who have reached the age of maturity will concern themselves with maintaining their own participation in this phase of the national vigor — national life."

An old American avocation, hero worship; advances in communications; and the development of a sedentary population has made many spectator sports into major industries. Television has played a tremendous hand in this geometric growth.

The magic of television has acted as a stimulus to sports event attendance and has not greatly affected gate receipts at the "live" event. Typical is the case of the New York Giants professional football team, which participated in a league television blackout arrangement. The television con-

Basketball game,
Harlem Globetrotters, Michigan.

177

*Water skier on slalom ski
at Cypress Gardens, Florida.*

Boston Red Sox baseball pitcher in motion.

*Central Park, urban
recreation area, New York.*

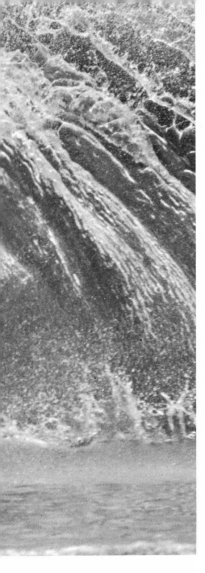

tract with the National Professional Football League specified that there would be no television of any game in that league within 50 miles of the city in which a game was being played.

Television coverage of the Giants' away games so intensified interest in the team that home games were consistently sold out. As a result, thousands of fans checked into hotels and motels out of town, facilities which had erected giant antennae to bring the game in from stations more than 50 miles from New York. The club owners have now drastically modified the blackout rule. The relationship of television and professional athletics was strengthened with the purchase, in 1966, of the New York Yankees baseball team by the Columbia Broadcasting System.

So successful has professional football been in this country that a star college athlete can set himself up for life by playing football. In 1965, the New York Jets of the American Football League paid star University of Alabama quarterback Joe Namath a reported $400,000 for signing.

The Namath story is a reflection of the rivalry between the young American League, formed for the 1960 season, and the more venerable National League, which traces its first kickoff to 1921. In order to assure top player material, the rival leagues had to bid against each other for talent. This problem will be solved for the leagues by their announced future merger, despite past strained relations. The merger will also bring about the scheduling of the first World Series of football between the top teams in each league.

College football, undoubtedly this country's most popular outdoor scholastic sport, came on the scene much earlier. In 1840 an annual series of freshman-sophomore scrimmages began at Yale. The first official intercollegiate game was between Princeton and Rutgers in New Brunswick, New Jersey, on November 6, 1869. Rutgers won six goals to four.

The football season culminates with the traditional Thanksgiving Day games between longtime rivals; the Yale-Harvard game; the Army-Navy game, which draws in excess of 100,000 fans to Philadelphia; and the bowl games, held about usually on New Year's Day. The most famous is the Rose Bowl game, which follows a civic parade of floral-decorated floats and draws 100,000 people to Pasadena's Rose Bowl, to see the top Pacific coast team tangle with the leading Midwestern eleven.

It was the enormous crowds drawn by college football that set the athletic department cash registers tinkling — and which today serve the important purpose of paying for most of the rest of the school's athletic program — usually subsidizing baseball, swimming, track and field, gymnastics, rowing, tennis, skiing, golf, boxing and wrestling.

In most cases, basketball pays its own way. In a number of small colleges noted for their basketball teams (and their acumen in acquiring student bodies with sufficient men over seven-feet tall), the game pays the way of the other sports. Basketball — college, professional, semi-professional and amateur — is America's most widely-attended indoor sport.

Of all the games that Americans play and watch, none is thought more typical of the country than baseball. The first game of baseball in history was played in 1839 at Cooperstown, New York. Abner Doubleday laid out the first baseball diamond for the cadets of the military school where he taught. The dimensions of the field set by Doubleday have remained the same to this day. In 1919, Cooperstown leased the ground where this first game was played and built the National Museum of Baseball and Hall of Fame, which contains names and memorabilia of the sport's past.

No game has ever produced such a mixed group and proliferation of heroes as has baseball. Few will argue that the greatest of them all was the late Babe Ruth, whose real name was George Herman Ruth. Ruth, a Baltimore urchin whose playing career spanned the years 1914 to 1935, established 27 major league records that have never been equalled. Ruth's most famous record is his 60 home run mark set during the 1927 season. It is a fact of baseball life that pitchers are poor hitters, but in Ruth's early career he was one of the most impressive pitchers in the game. A left-hander, he won 92 games and lost 44 in his pitching years — 1914 to 1933 — although he pitched only during 11 of those years. In 1916 and 1917 he won 23 games each season.

The great Ruth days began in 1920, when he was sold by the Boston Red Sox to the New York Yankees for $125,000. He remained with the Yankees until 1934, spending his last active playing year with the Boston National League team. So great was Ruth as an attraction that when Yankee Stadium was built it was nicknamed "The House that Ruth Built."

Although Yankee Stadium epitomized the baseball park of the Ruth-Lou Gehrig era, one of the new wonders of the national pastime is the vast Astrodome, home of the Houston Astros baseball team. Being completely enclosed, it is the only stadium in which games can be played, conventions held and special entertainment provided in any weather and at any season of the year. Its mammoth air conditioning plant, plastic roof and synthetic grass amaze even the most blasé visitor.

Golf has the peculiar quality of attracting both amateurs and professionals. It is such a combination of spectating and participating, that it is almost impossible to separate the two approaches to it. Golf professionals go on annual tours, playing such famous tourneys as the Masters at the Augusta National Golf Club in Georgia, the National Open and the Professional Golfers' Association contests. The top men in professional golf win prize money which can mean more than $100,000 per year to such top-ranking pros as Jack Nicklaus, Gary Player, Arnold Palmer and Billy Casper. Amateur golf also enjoys a fantastic popularity in the United States. The golf course, at the country club level, remains one of the greatest excuses for doing business, exercising and keeping physically fit.

The late President Kennedy's plea for greater participation by all the people in physical fitness activities should not be equated with the multi-millions of dollars spent annually on commercialized spectator sports. For the average man, participation in both sports and physical fitness activity has to be confined to non-superman activities — those that require a minimum number of competitors and a minimum outlay for equipment and playing facilities.

It is not at all surprising, therefore, that those few remaining sports which are still nearly 100 per cent amateur, are those which can be engaged in by one to four persons, using very little special equipment—track and field, swimming, handball, gymnastics and fencing, to name but a few. Most of these, and other largely amateur sports, are usually as close as the local YMCA, Boy's Club or other local sports-recreation center.

Modern Americans need organized play. Our technology has cut the physical exertion of earning the daily bread to almost zero. Most Americans sit on their way to work, during work and on the way home. The time for leisure has increased as the working hours have decreased to about 35 to 40 hours per week. But the modern American has found practical means of using this extra time. The pioneer spirit, far from dead, has kept alive this competitive urge. Therefore, America in sports is indeed

Playing field, Houston Astrodome.

America at play.

No brief compendium can express the overall spectrum of America at play and include every sport, every pastime, every hobby, every form of recreation, every do-it-yourself activity. Nowhere else on the face of the earth are there people who have so much leisure and, therefore, time to play as in this treasured land. Not because it is so large or so prosperous, but because it continues to grow, to experiment, to adapt, to innovate. One source lists 73 associations dedicated to the pursuit of various athletic activities — from the Amateur Athletic Union of the United States to the World Boxing Association and including such unique organizations as the American Roque League and the National Duck Pin Bowling Congress.

There are also amateur-professional occupations such as horse racing, dog racing, harness racing and many others. These sports are largely sponsored by amateurs, but the conditioning of the animals involved is usually the job of professionals. However, a number of activities represent the highly affluent American at play — International cup yacht racing, polo, Indianapolis-style auto racing and riding to hounds.

Auto racing has bred the Indianapolis 500 Mile Race on Memorial Day, sponsored by auto manufacturers and suppliers of parts and fuel. This and other such events have contributed to the development of automobile engineering improvements. From the American basic urge to tinker, has come the new breed of youngsters who buy an ancient car, completely re-build its engine and come out with an ultra-speedy "hot rod" that confounds the professional Detroit mechanics.

Certain cities and institutions of learning are intimately associated with certain sports, but often there is no way to account for this. Several examples make the point clear. Rowing: The University of Washington, Seattle. Almost without exception collegiate rowing coaches of the United States are alumni of Washington. Adult amateurs in the field of rowing, however, look to the banks of the Schuykill River in Philadelphia and its Victorian boat houses. One of its dedicated amateur scullers was John B. Kelly, originally a bricklayer, but the first American single sculler to win the coveted event at the British Henley regatta in the 1920's. Lacrosse: the old Canadian-Indian game of baggataway is now associated, for no apparent reason, with Baltimore, but is played enthusiastically by amateurs all over the country. Swimming: Yale is the place to go if you're a swimmer. Bob Kipputh, probably the greatest collegiate swimming coach in our history, made it that way. Winter Sports: Dartmouth College, Hanover, New Hampshire, where the students ski or snowshoe to classes in the winter.

Then, all kinds of animals — dogs, horses, cats and cattle — are shown in a number of ways. A "best of show" *can* be selected from a simple house pet at the Westminster Kennel Club Show in Madison Square Garden, New York — the World Series of dogdom. More often a dog owned by a professional or semi-professional breeder, rarely seen by the owner, and brought into condition and shown by a professional handler, more frequently makes the star ranks.

A new sport, sky-diving — jumping out of an airplane with a parachute, executing certain maneuvers, delaying opening of the 'chute' as long as possible and then hitting a target with a bullseye in the center-is becoming increasingly popular.

Bowling is one of our most popular and readily available amateur sports. Originally called nine-pins, it came under severe criticism as a game for ruffians and was restricted or banned by law in certain communities, especially on Sundays. Ingeniously, a pin was added, thus making ten pins which evaded the law and created the modern game.

Perhaps the purest form of American sports amateurism is expressed in the Amateur Athletic Union and Olympic teams. Not only is this simon-pure amateurism jealously guarded, but the contestants behave accordingly. One of our greatest female backstroke swimming stars, Eleanor Holm, was dropped from the U. S. Olympic team for sipping champagne on the ship taking her to the 1932 games in Berlin.

The word sports of course, doesn't tell the full story of America at

(Continued on page 187)

Stern-wheel excursion boat, Mississippi River.

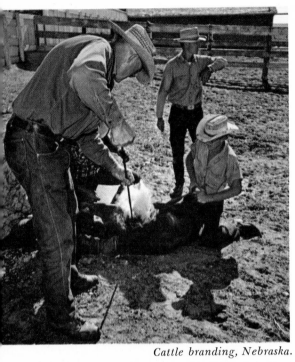

Cattle branding, Nebraska.

Sailing, southern tip of New Jersey.

South side of Chicago.

Blessing of the Animals, southern California.

Seminole Indians, southern Florida.

Thunderhead over Ft. Lauderdale, Florida.

Small town, Kansas

Hunter, northern Wisconsin.

Russian Hill, San Francisco.

Chicago River at night.

New York subway.

Southern California coast.

play. The key word for much of the story is recreation.

Recreation can mean swimming at beaches, playing contract bridge, gin rummy, pinochle or poker. It can mean games like chess, checkers, Monopoly or even Scrabble. Recreation can be charades at a small party or bingo in a crowded hall. It can mean indulging in countless hobbies and do-it-yourself projects. It can be a springtime game of marbles by youngsters at New York's Central Park or a day-long assault on a one-armed bandit slot machine by little old ladies in the gaudy precincts of Las Vegas.

From the Boston Common, our first public playground set up in 1633, to such modern concepts as the Cape Cod National Seashore, governments — city, state, and federal — have been acquiring land, improving or restoring it and turning it back to the people. The nation's largest area of this kind — a boon to hikers, campers, picnickers, motorists, power and sail boat enthusiasts – is Lake Mead Recreation Area in Arizona and Nevada, which comprises nearly two million acres.

In sports and recreation lie the fulfillment of many of the noblest aspirations of our people. The roar of the crowd at a ball park; the plunk of a golf ball into a cup surrounded by a closely manicured carpet of green grass; tulips nodding gently in a city park on a sunny May morning; the chilling call of a loon across a majestic, cliff-shrouded lake — in places such as these is the challenge and beauty of recreation and of the open spaces for all our people.

The Wonder of American Cities

There is a phenomenon occurring twice a day in America, about 7:30 or 8 o'clock in the morning and again about 5 o'clock. Restless people by the millions start their cars and board trains or subways or buses. There are a wealthy few who walk up the ramp of an airliner or clamber into their private plane or helicopter.

The rush is on, the invasion of the city or the exodus to its environs as much as 50 miles away depends upon the time of day. This is commuting, and nearly everyone has learned a new patience in the midst of a traffic snarl on highways which never seem to be adequately large or while standing in the human jam aboard a bus or subway. But in most cities the phenomenon is even more striking. Urban workers choose suburbs or even rural areas perhaps as far away as another state in which to live, and the city dwellers move from their apartments to factories and offices in the perimeter communities.

Our cities are the most vivid, bright, noisy and exciting in the world. They literally tremble with the dynamic people and businesses which are their mainstream and with the endless thunder of the builders. Somehow it has seemed until very recently that there are few exceptions to the rule of the family which chooses to work there won't live there, and the man who lives there finds employment miles away. But now there is the beginning of a trend to live and work in the city.

Even a partial roster of American cities is impressive: Boston, with its sense of history and outstanding educational and research institutions; New

Orleans Street, French Quarter, New Orleans.

Busch Memorial Stadium and Gateway Arch, St. Louis.

York, the communications, fashion, financial and theatre center of the nation; Philadelphia, suffused with recollections of proud, vital moments of history; Washington, D.C., comfortable-looking, without skyscrapers, but throbbing underneath the surface as the political power center of the free world; Miami, towering with the luxury hotels that the supremely affluent nation requires for its leisure; Atlanta, bursting with all the recently acquired accouterments of a major metropolis, the capital city of the new South; New Orleans, with its world-famous restaurants, the last vestige of French heritage in the urban United States; Detroit, the automobile manufacturing center of the nation and the world; Chicago, with its beautiful lakefront and always bustling activity; Milwaukee, where most of the country's breweries are located, retaining its Germanic flavor; Minneapolis-St. Paul, the "Twin Cities," as progressive as any metropolitan area in the nation; St. Louis, with its Old World charm and urban renaissance; Kansas City, surprising first visitors with its beauty, wealth and culture; Houston, fast becoming the space headquarters for the nation and the focus of the legends of Texas oil wealth; Denver, strikingly nestled in the foothills of the Rockies with its envied climate; Seattle, a major location of the burgeoning aircraft industry; San Francisco, the city to which many Americans would like to move, so greatly respected is the quality of its life; and finally, Los Angeles, with its movie-makers, informal living, freeways and newly displayed involvement in the arts.

There are the stately town houses overlooking San Francisco Bay, fashionable mansions on Boston's Beacon Hill and elegant residences set amidst century-old homes in New York City's best sections. These areas and others, such as Chicago's "Old Town," which had been allowed to run down and have now been refurbished, are part of the reason for the movement of people back to the city. But there is a more important factor.

As enormous funds are being spent for construction of single-family homes in suburbia, now great amounts of money are also poured into cities which have exerted mammoth efforts to rebuild. Thousands of luxury apartments have been constructed, often above the rubble remaining after bulldozers leveled slum areas or erased forever tired-looking brownstones, considered the fashionable place to live when America was lighted with gas.

Often these apartments are a complete city within one or two buildings rising 30, 40 or even 50 stories. Swimming pools, health clubs, markets, underground parking lots, private wine cellars and specialty shops are included in many of them. It is conceivable a child could come home to an apartment complex such as this after birth and remain there until he dies, leaving only for a place of final rest.

Retirement is coming earlier each year, and many still relatively young couples with grown children have sold their suburban homes for a return to the cities whence they came. It is often these very luxury apartments which draw them back to a life of elegant leisure only a short walk from fine restaurants and theatres.

To many younger Americans, more days of commuting mean more

expense, which can be avoided by moving back to the cities. A significant and enormous billboard rises high above the lines of traffic funneling into one of Boston's major intersections, and pointedly enough it is set upon the lawn of high-rise, luxury apartments open only a few months. Doubtlessly many drivers choking in the traffic soot and already tired from a long day ponder twice when they read: "If you lived here, you'd be home now."

But there is another side to the apartment dwellers. Millions upon millions of apartments in American cities are not quite as sumptuous as the luxury urban homes. Many Americans live in them because they are adequate homes and within the financial means of their inhabitants. They comprise the vast majority of urban dwellings. Old, yes, but clean, inexpensive and convenient.

Then, there are the deadly slums, often the homes of the elderly who have lived there since childhood and watched their neighborhood diminish in attractiveness. In many cases these are the homes of minority groups, held in ghettoes that they or their parents may have originally formed for self-assurance and mutual assistance in a strange land or unfamiliar part of the nation. While America's slums are an undeniable fact, these conditions fortunately are being rectified with massive Federal programs to rehabilitate substandard housing or replace it with homes equal to the dignity of man.

It must also be noted that while some ethnic communities are located in slum areas, many others are neat, clean and prosperous, frequently having lower crime rates than some of the wealthier suburbs. In fact, the entire American community is made up of nothing but ethnic strains of varying degrees of purity and diffuseness, and the entire range of the nation's accomplishments, as well as its weaknesses, must be attributed to the descendants of immigrants. America is a nation of immigrants in the sense that the ancestors of all Americans, except the American Indians, came to these shores within the past 400 years.

The vast majority of immigrants — 35 million — came from Europe; 5.6 million came from the Americas, 1.1 million from the rest of the world. This immigration differed from the migrations of peoples earlier in world history in that it was and is a movement of families and individuals rather than nations, races and clans. Most of them came as a result of economic forces.

The so-called "old immigration" was almost entirely Anglo-Saxon-Celtic in nature. It was peasant in origin and primarily agricultural and land-owning in intention. The Scandinavians and Germans who came shortly after the Civil War continued this trend. But the possibility of absorbing immigration on the land had come substantially to an end by 1890, just a few years after the beginning of the so-called "new immigration." Much of this immigration was of agricultural origin but was drawn into the cities in America by a lack of land and the high wages in the rapidly expanding industrial and mining centers in the East and Midwest. These immigrants came mainly from central, eastern and southern Europe. They — along with the Negroes, Mexicans and the Puerto Ricans, who have migrated to American cities primarily since World War II — are the pre-

Train tracks, La Salle Street Station, Chicago.

Commuters, Grand Central Station, New York.

dominant ethnic groups in American cities. The Chinese have lived in the cities for many decades.

The cities' older sections — three-decker homes, row houses bequeathed by mill owners, but maintained by the descendants of mill workers — frequently are the strongholds of these ethnic groups in our great industrial cities across the land. In Boston, for example, the colorful North End, East Boston, across the harbor, with its pungent Italian restaurants and militant neighborhood loyalties, its seasonal parades in honor of patron saints, can readily be compared with similar neighborhoods on the East Side of New York, with well-known areas of Denver and certainly with the "Little Italies" of San Francisco and other sections of California.

The ethnic communities endure and prosper along with the abundant life resplendent about it: the Chinese in Boston, New York, San Francisco, overflowing with restaurants and commerce, and their young making fine reputations in science, mathematics and architecture; the Mexicans in Los Angeles, carrying on their rich customs; the Poles of Chicago, Detroit and Milwaukee, still clustered together in certain areas, despite their educational and financial status; the Germans of Milwaukee, Cincinnati; the Swedes, Danes, Norwegians of Minneapolis and the Minnesota farmlands and steel-smelting areas, all in a certain national togetherness, characteristic of our "melting pot," but still stubbornly Europe-touched land.

The might and splendor of the Jewish-American participation in government, art and business has produced such names as Justice Louis Brandeis, Ambassador Arthur Goldberg, composer-conductor Leonard Bernstein, who swell our nation's justified pride in its immigrant origins. Irish mayors in

Street conversation in Harlem, New York.

Italian butcher shop, Boston.

Boston, German mayors in Milwaukee, French mayors in Woonsocket, Rhode Island and New Orleans, and Italian and Polish cabinet members are not unusual occurrences. And, around the bend, in the wondrous irrepressible democracy of our land which saw an Irish-Catholic, John F. Kennedy, elected President of the United States in 1960, is more change, and the further ascendancy of ethnic groups into predictable areas of power and wealth. The emergence of the American Negro is well upon our culture, the irony being that the free American colored man has been a native citizen for about 15 generations.

This is what American cities are: people from the very rich to the very poor, each moving day by day for his pleasure and survival. The city is a place of extraordinary wealth and unbelievable poverty. But each member of all these classes, despite his surroundings, can arise each day with some anticipation of what it will bring, knowing that, whatever his problems, freedom is his ultimate resource.

A city in America is like a woodland pond to a farm boy: It can be either just an area different from its perimeter or a magical place holding all the wonders of the universe if its beholder only takes a few moments to peer at it closely and explore its depths with a calculating eye. The glitter is only as iridescent as the perception of the man who sees it.

Cityscape of natural and man-created elements, Chicago.